I0119334

The **GAME DAY™**

POKER ALMANAC™

OFFICIAL RULES
OF POKER

The Game Day Poker Almanac Official Rules of Poker is the first
book in the Game Day Poker Almanac series. Each year, Game Day
publishes the Poker Almanac as a complete reference guide for the
poker player and the poker-industry professional.

Watch for the 2008 Poker Almanac from Game Day
in Spring 2008.

Volume discounts for qualified groups and organizations are available.
Professional discounts are available for licensed poker dealers and poker-industry professionals.

Call Game Day at 303-375-0499 for more inforemaiton on these discount,
or write to Game Day, Poker Almanac, 18601 Green Valely Ranch Blvd, Suite
112, No. 4, Denver, Colorado 80249.

For more information about Game Day and the Poker Almanac series,
visit www.FlyingPenPress.com/GameDay

The GAME DAY™ POKER ALMANAC™

OFFICIAL RULES OF POKER

KELLI MIX

GAME DAY™
GAME BOOKS AND BOOKS ABOUT GAMES

an imprint of

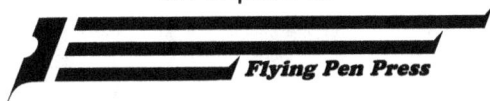

Flying Pen Press

The Game Day Poker Almanac Official Rules of Poker
The poker rulebook of the Game Day Poker Almanac series, shelve in Poker.
Published by Game Day.
First Edition, continuous printing on demand, first date of publication June 2007.

Author & Editor: Kelli Mix, Editor.PokerRules@FlyingPenPress.com
Back Cover Photograph: Tim McClain, www.mccphotos.com

ISBN: 978-0-9795889-2-1

Game Day is an imprint of
Flying Pen Press LLC
18601 Green Valley Ranch Blvd., Suite 112 No. 4
Denver CO 80249
www.FlyingPenPress.com/GameDay

All Flying Pen Press titles, imprints, and distributed lines are available at special quantity discounts for bulk purchases for sales promotion, premiums, fund raising, educational or institutional use.

The Game Day Poker Almanac Official Rules of Poker text copyright ©2007 Kelli Mix.
Robert's Rules of Poker and Robert's Rules of Poker for Private Games copyright ©2007 Bob Ciaffone.
The Poker Tournament Directors Association Rules copyright ©2007 Poker Tournament Directors Association.
World Series of Poker Rules copyright ©2007 World Series of Poker.
Compilation and cover design copyright ©2007 Flying Pen Press LLC.

All rights reserved. No part of this book may be reproduced in any form or by any means without the express written consent of the publisher, excepting brief quotes used in reviews. For permission to reproduce any part or the whole of this book, contact the publisher.

Poker Almanac, the "spade in circle" logo, Game Day, "Game Books and Books about Games," the stylized "GD" logo, Flying Pen Press, and the flying pen nub logos are trademarks of Flying Pen Press LLC. World Series of Poker is a registered trademark of Harrah's License Company LLC. World Poker Tour is a registered trademark of WPT Enterprises, Inc.

Manufactured in the United States of America and in the United Kingdom.
Printing by Lightning Source Inc. and Lightning Source UK Limited.

Laws regarding gambling and the playing of poker for monetary wagers vary greatly from location to location. Neither the publisher nor the author condone such activity where it is illegal. This book gives rules for the game of poker as it is played in casinos and cardrooms, where allowed by law and/or licensed by local and national gaming authorities. This book is not intended to give legal advice, and anyone intending to play poker for monetary wagers is strongly advised to consult with a licensed attorney.

While this book provides rules and structure for poker playing, readers should be aware that there is no obligation for any poker room to adhere to any of the rules given in this book, and that poker rooms must use rules that comply with local laws and gaming regulations. Poker players who play for monetary wagers are strongly advised to read each poker facility's in-house poker rulebook.

Readers who play poker for monetary wagers do so at their own risk; neither the publisher nor the author assume any responsibility for wagers lost in games of poker.

Know your limits, and play for fun. If you or someone you know has a gambling problem, contact the National Council on Problematic Gambling at 1-800-522-4700.

CONTENTS

ACKNOWLEDGMENTS

I would like to acknowledge Bob Ciaffone for writing *Robert's Rules of Poker* and providing feedback on the Elements of Poker. Thank you to Matt Savage, Linda Johnson, David Lamb and Jan Fisher for starting the Poker Tournament Directors Association. All five of these people have volunteered their time and provided their rules solely to improve the game of poker. I am grateful to Bob Daily and Gary Thompson for granting permission to print the World Series of Poker rules.

Thank you to my publisher, David Rozansky, who worked with me on a handshake and smile for many months before finally forcing me to sign a contract. The following people provided feedback, proofreading and poker advice throughout this project; to each of them I am indebted: Richard Mix, David and Phillissa Rozansky, Debra Forthman, Aaron Alberts, Toby Bell, Brian Walsingham and Kip Williams. I am most appreciative of the help of writer Jay Alberts who provided endless amounts of proofreading, writing advice and much needed humor.

Thanks to all the guys I play poker with for never making me feel like the girl who ruined "boy's night out": Aaron, Al, All-in Glenn, Billy, Bobby, Buddy, Cartwright, Cary Wray, Chris, Constantine, Cotton, Eric the Snatch-o-ppotamus, George, Gerald, Jody, Joey, John River Rat, Johnny, Josh, Kip, Larry, Lee, Lightning, Little David, Mike, Mr. Dickey, Razorblade, Rhudy, Rickey, Terry, Toby, Tubby and Trey. We may yell, call each other names, and occasionally throw cards at one another, but one, two, sometimes three days later, I still call each one of them my friend.

My family has been very supportive of me even at times when it is hard to support a poker playing soccer mom. I am grateful to Lyle and Judy for helping me meet deadlines by entertaining the wild ones.

Thanks to my husband, Richard, who encourages me to play poker even during the worst losing streaks. He is responsible for me working on this book and after eleven years, he remains my number one fan. I owe a debt of gratitude to my sister Stacey who brings out the best in me. I am also indebted to my other siblings, Amber, Laura and Sean for years of crumpled cards, overturned tables and broken board games — the experience was invaluable. I am grateful to my parents Randy and Gloria for reminding us that winning isn't everything…unless we are at the Bowman family reunion.

Finally, thank you to Katie and Cheyenne Mix for dancing in the kitchen, singing in the bathtub and jumping on the bed with me until I forget every bad beat.

The **GAME DAY™**

POKER ALMANAC™

OFFICIAL RULES OF POKER

INTRODUCTION

A few years ago I sat down in a 5/10 no-limit Texas Hold 'Em game with a rack of chips. I positioned five $100 bills in front of me and placed each stack of chips on top of them. I lost two stacks within an hour before flopping a lock straight against two aggressive opponents.

"Excellent," I thought as one opponent bet and one raised.

"Raise," I said confidently, counting my bills and placing them out front for the dealer.

"Sorry," said the dealer, pushing the cash back to me. "Cash does not play."

I was surprised by this rule, as it is common practice to bet cash or chips in most casino games I was accustomed to playing. I was also angry; angry at both dealers for not pointing this out to me while the cash was in front of me for close to an hour, and especially angry at myself for not asking up front if cash played. The players continued betting into a side pot which I was not eligible to win although I had five hundred dollars in front of me. It was mistake that cost me an extra $1,000.

This oversight by myself and the dealers exemplified that the rules of poker vary so much from game to game. I decided I would write a book on the rules of poker so that I could establish a definitive set of poker rules which every cardroom could follow. This was extremely presumptuous. As I began to research casino rules, speak with tournament directors and study publications it quickly became apparent to me that it is not possible for every casino to adhere to one set of rules.

Regional and state-by-state legal differences make it impossible for all cardrooms to follow the exact same set of rules. Despite these challenges it still remains possible for all cardrooms to share a common base set of rules. Many cardroom managers have used Bob Ciaffone's *Robert's Rules of Poker* as the foundation for rules specific to their cardroom with adjustments to meet legal guidelines and rules that specifically apply to that cardroom.

The same holds true for tournaments. Many tournament directors follow the rules established by the Poker Tournament Directors Association (TDA) and make necessary adjustments based on legal and customary elements.

The World Series of Poker is an ideal example of the evolution of creating poker rules. Management took a combination of *Robert's Rules of Poker* and the TDA rules, incorporated these rules with the Nevada Gaming Commission regulations as well as specific WSOP considerations and developed their existing ninety-three rules.

The foundation for such rules is provided in this book. Chapter One describes the basic elements of poker from the standard flow of a cardroom to playing out a hand of poker. Chapter Two includes *Robert's Rules of Poker* for casinos and private games, the Poker Tournament Directors Association rules and the World Series of Poker player rules. Chapter Three provides a detailed description of etiquette rules that should be followed in every poker game. Chapter Four gives specific step-by-step directions for the most popular variant poker games.

It is my hope that this book will persuade cardroom managers, as well as the host of any card game, to move in a positive direction toward standardizing poker rules. I encourage management to look at existing rules and find a way to unify them with the professional rules in this book. I also challenge all poker players to request a copy of cardroom rules, ask questions, make suggestions and never hesitate to ask, "Does cash play?"

— Kelli Mix

CHAPTER ONE

ELEMENTS OF POKER

Introduction to Poker

This chapter provides a clear understanding of how a common cardroom is run as well as the basic elements of any poker game. This information is not only essential to a beginning player, but also provides the details necessary for creating customized cardroom rules for every poker game.

Definition of Poker

Poker is a card game with a strong element of skill played by two or more players that follow a set ranking of hands upon which players bet the value of their hand. One or more players win money or chips in a central pot based on any one or combination of the following criteria:

- The pot or prize is awarded to or split between the holders of a hand of cards ranked in some way that all players have agreed upon.
- The pot or prize is awarded to or split between the holders of the best poker hand as represented by five cards, with at least one card that is personal and unknown to all the other players.
- The pot or prize is awarded to or split between bettors who have placed a bet in the pot that other players have chosen to not match.

Player Objective

Each player in the game attempts to make the best poker hand in order to win the pot. Poker hands are valued according to the game: highest rank games, wildcard rank games and lowest rank games.

Hand Rankings

All poker games follow a standard system of ranking hands in order to determine the winner of each hand. Most cardrooms use the high-hand ranking system to determine the winning hand in a poker game. The wild card high-hand rankings are normally not used in professional cardrooms, but can be found in many home games. The low-hand ranking is used in cardrooms predominantly in high-low split games with an eight-high qualifier, and is used often in variant home games. In games using the low-hand ranking, the best hand is the hand with the lowest rank.

Ranking of High Poker Hands

The high-hand poker ranking system has been used since the advent of poker and remains the ranking of choice in poker games. There is never a deviation from this ranking in cardrooms and it is the system most poker players adhere to. The hands are ranked as follows with the highest rank listed first:

Royal flush   10♣J♣Q♣K♣A♣

An ace-high straight flush. There is not a higher ranking royal flush. Two royal flushes tie for highest rank hand.

Straight flush   6♥7♥8♥9♥10♥

Five suited cards in sequential rank order. Aces count as a low card in an ace-to-five straight flush. The highest card in the straight flush decides the highest rank. For example, 6♥7♥8♥9♥10♥ beats 4♠5♠6♠7♠8♠.

Four-of-a-kind   8♠8♣8♥8♦A♦

A hand containing four cards of the same rank with one unrelated card. The rank of the four matching cards decides which four-of-a-kind is higher. For example 8♠8♣8♥8♦A♦ beats 7♠7♣7♥7♦A♥.

Full house   Q♠Q♣Q♥4♥4♦

Three cards of the same rank with two cards of another matching rank. The rank of the three matching cards decides which full house is higher. For example, Q♠Q♣Q♥4♥4♦ beats 8♠8♣8♥A♥A♠. Ties are decided by the rank of the other two matching cards.

Flush   K♦3♦7♦9♦2♦

Any five cards of the same suit. The highest card in the flush determines the higher rank, with ties decided by the next highest card. For example, 3♠5♠7♠Q♠K♠ beats 3♥5♥6♥Q♥K♥.

Straight   6♠7♣8♥9♥10♦

Five various suited cards in sequential rank order. Aces count as a low card in an ace to five straight. The highest card in the straight decides the highest rank. For example, 6♠7♣8♥9♥10♥ beats 5♠6♣7♥8♠9♦.

Three-of-a-kind   9♠9♣9♥J♦Q♣

Three cards of the same rank with two unrelated cards of various rank and suit. The rank of the three matching cards decides which three-of-a-kind is higher. Ties are decided by the higher rank of the unrelated cards. For example, in a tied hand where community cards are shared, 9♠9♣9♥Q♠J♥ beats 9♠9♣9♦J♥7♠.

Two pairs   2♣2♦A♦A♠7♥

Two cards of matching rank with two other cards of another matching rank and one unrelated card. The higher rank of the paired cards decides the higher of the two pairs. For example, J♠J♥4♣4♠K♣ beats 9♠9♥10♥10♠K♦. Ties are decided by the lower denomination of paired cards and further decided by the rank of the fifth unrelated card.

One pair   K♥K♣7♠8♥9♦

Two cards of the same rank and three unrelated cards of various rank and suit. The higher rank of the paired cards decides the highest hand. For example, K♥K♣7♠8♥9♦ beats J♠J♣4♦5♦A♥. Ties are decided by the highest rank of the unrelated cards followed by the second highest and finally the lowest rank of the unrelated cards.

High card   4♠7♠9♦J♥A♣

No pairs and five unrelated cards of various rank and suit. The card with the highest rank determines the highest hand. Ties are decided by the second highest rank, followed by the third, fourth and finally the lowest rank card. For example, A♣J♥9♦7♠4♠ beats A♥J♣9♥6♣4♦.

Ranking of Poker Hands with Wild Cards

The wild card ranking of poker hands follows the same structure as the high-hand rankings with one standard addition: five-of-a-kind is the best possible hand. This ranking system is used mostly in home games and is often altered to accommodate even more variant hands. The wild card represents any card that best completes the poker hand.

Five-of-a-kind   9♣9♥9♠9♦W

Four cards of the same rank with one wild card which represents the same rank. The rank of the five matching cards decides which five-of-a-kind is higher. For example 9♣9♥9♠9♦W beats 8♠8♣8♥8♦W.

Ranking of Low Poker Hands

The low ranking of poker hands is used in various forms of lowball, or low poker, as well as in high-low split pot games. The hand ranking is in the reverse order of the high-hand ranking system. The best hand is the lowest rank. There are three common hand ranking systems for low games: ace to five, ace to six and deuce to seven. In addition, many games, especially high-low split games, use an eight-high qualifier when determining a low hand, which means in order to qualify for the low hand players must have no card higher than an eight in their hand.

Another common difference in low-hand ranking is whether an ace counts as a high or low card and if straights and flushes count against a low hand. These clarifications should be made in the cardroom rulebook for any game using a low-hand ranking system.

Ace to Five Low

The best possible hand is a five-high straight regardless of suit (A♥2♥3♥4♥5♥). The ace always counts as a low card and straights and flushes *do not count* against a low hand.

Ace to Six Low

The best possible hand is six-high hand of various rank and suit (A♠2♣3♣4♦6♥). The ace always counts as a low card and straights and flushes *do count* against a low hand.

Deuce to Seven Low

The best possible hand is a seven-high hand of various rank and suit (2♠3♦4♦5♥7♠). The ace always counts as a high card and straights and flushes *do count* against a low hand.

The Cardroom

The House

The house refers to the casino, company, organization or person that is hosting the poker game. The goal of the house, like any business, is to make money. The best way to make money is to provide an atmosphere that is comfortable, welcoming and secure. A successful house will be inviting to new players while maintaining a reputable business that keeps players coming back on a regular basis.

Announcing Rules

The rules of conduct and play vary from cardroom to cardroom. Most cardrooms post the rules for players to read, others provide copies that may be obtained at the front desk. Even in a casual home game, if money is involved, it is important to establish rules and to provide a written copy of those rules to any player upon request. This will protect both the house and the players from problems that may arise from inconsistent rules. Bob Ciaffone's *Robert's Rules of Poker*, found in Chapter Two, is a complete and comprehensive list of poker rules that can be modified to meet the needs of any cardroom.

Duration of Play

The cardroom manager or houseperson should always let players know what time a game will start and end. In a casino, games will typically start as soon as there are enough players to start a table and continue for as long as the players wish to play. In home games, there is usually a predetermined start-time and the game begins as soon as enough players fill the table after that time. The houseperson in a home game should always announce the time the game will end. If there is no set end-time, the houseperson should give some advance notice, such as, "We will play for one more hour," or, "Two more rounds of play and the game will end."

The House Money

The two common methods the house uses for charging players to play in a poker game is a rake or a set fee.

A Raked Game

In a raked game the dealer takes chips out of the pot during each hand of play. The amount taken varies per game, but typically a minimum amount of money must be in the pot before a dealer may extract the rake and there is a maximum set amount per hand that a dealer may take.

Table Fee

In a game with a fee, players are charged a fixed amount that they must pay to the dealer for a set period of time such as every half-hour or hour. Typically, when a new dealer comes to the table, he or she will announce "Time," and all players will place a chip(s) out front to cover the fee amount. The dealer will collect the money, ensuring that every player has paid. If a player is away from the table at collection time, the dealer will take the fee from his or her chip stack. The dealer will then drop the total amount of chips into a drop box. Some casinos require the dealer to announce the total amount to the floorperson before dropping the chips.

Banking – Buying Chips

Most poker games use chips in place of actual money in order to speed up the game. Players may go directly to the cashier cage and exchange money for chips. The cashier does not know which game a player will be playing; therefore, the player must request the specific denomination of chips needed. It is important to know the minimum buy-in amount and have a general idea of the average chip count at the table before buying chips. Most limit games require players to buy in for at least ten times the maximum bet.

Most cardrooms will offer the services of a chip runner, a person who will take money and exchange it at the cashier cage and return to the table with chips. In this situation, a player may sit down and place money on the table. The dealer will call for a chip runner and usually provide a small number of chips while the player is waiting for additional chips. The dealer must announce to the table how many chips the player "has behind the hand," so other players are aware of how many chips are at risk.

Cash at the Table

Cash, in addition to chips, is permitted in certain poker games. Higher stakes games will typically allow players to place cash behind or under their chips for additional betting ammunition. Players may buy and sell chips amongst themselves in a cash-permitted game. The use of cash in lieu of chips tends to slow the poker game down and makes it harder for players to recognize the amount of money at risk. In order to help with this, the cash typically must be in specific increments and the total amount made available to any player upon request. All players should know what denominations of currency can play. When cash is bet, the dealer should always count the bills and announce the betting amount even if the bettor has already done so.

Table Stakes

A common rule that states a player is never permitted to add money or chips to the table while a hand is in play, is referred to as "table stakes." With the exception of a rare home game, table stakes is enforced in all poker games; otherwise, players could wait for a lock hand and add money to increase the size of the pot. A player may purchase additional chips or add money to the table at anytime before or after an active hand. A player is never permitted to remove chips from the table unless he or she is leaving the game.

The Equipment

Value of Chips/Tokens

A standard casino chip has the value of the chip printed on both sides for easy identification. When the chip value is not printed on the face of the chip, it is necessary to clarify how much money each chip represents. A typical method for distinguishing chip values is by declaring a monetary value for each chip by color.

Commonly Used Poker Chip Colors and Values

White:	$1.00
Red:	$5.00
Blue:	$10.00
Green:	$25.00
Black:	$100.00
Purple	$500.00

The Deck

A standard deck of cards has 52 cards with four 13-card suits, including spades, hearts, diamonds and clubs. Every game should have at least two decks (one set-up) at the table for the dealer to use. The two decks should be differentiated by separate designs or colors on the backs of the cards. Any wild cards added to the deck should be announced at the start of the game.

The Dealer and the Players

The Dealer

In a casino setting the dealer is an employee hired to deal cards. The dealer is paid an hourly rate by the casino; however, the dealer makes most of his or her income through tips received from players. A small round disk, known as a dealer button, is used to indicate the designated dealer when using an employed dealer. The dealer in a cardroom is not permitted to play during the game and is required to maintain control of the poker table at all times. If a dealer is unable to resolve a dispute, the floorperson is called to the table for a definitive decision.

Home games often do not provide a dealer; players must take turns dealing the cards. It is common for each player to deal one hand then pass the cards to the player to the left for the next deal. Another option is to allow each person to deal a complete rotation before passing the deal to the next player. The host should establish whether dealers have the option to play while dealing. This tends to slow down the game, but does help keep a short-handed game active.

Tipping the Dealer

It is customary for the winning player(s) to give an employed dealer a tip, usually a small percentage of the pot, after the pot has been pushed. In home games, where the dealer is often one of the players, it is improper to tip the dealer.

Setting up the Deck

At the start of a game or whenever a new deck is introduced in the game, it should be set up in a specific order. The cards should be in suited order of spades, hearts, diamonds and clubs from the ace to the king.

The dealer typically takes the cards from the packaging, fans them out face-down, inspects the cards for irregularities, counts them, then turns them face-up in the ordered fan making sure no card is duplicated or missing and that no extraneous card is present, such as a joker or promotional card.

Seating Positions in a Live Game

Players select seats in a live poker game on a first-come-first-served basis up to the allowable number of players per game. Only the house dealer is assigned a seat, which is in the center position of the table.

The seats are numbered clockwise from the dealer. For example, the seat immediately to the left of the house dealer is the "one seat," to the left of that seat is the "two seat," and numbering continues around the table. The number of seats at a table is typically determined by the type of game being played. Community card games usually allow up to ten players, draw and stud games allow up to seven players. Once a table is full, players must request their name be put on a waitlist and wait to be called when an open seat becomes available.

Seat Changes

A player may request a seat change at the table at any time. If all the seats are currently occupied, the dealer will typically toss a seat change button to the player. A player requesting a seat change takes precedence over a player on the waitlist for that table. Once a seat is available, the player will return the seat change button to the dealer and switch to the open seat. A new player joining the table will then take the original seat of the player who switched seats.

Table Changes

Players may ask to be moved to another table with open seating as long as that person is not already at the main table in a "must move" game. If a seat is not available on the table in which the player is eligible to move, the player must get on the waitlist for that table. A player moving to another table of the same game must also move the same amount of money/chips.

Reserved Seat

Players are usually permitted a break from the table for an allotted amount of time, such as up to two dealer rounds. The houseperson/floorperson will remove the player's money/chips from the table if the player does not return within the allotted time. Some cardrooms will allow another player to play over a reserved seat until the player returns.

High Card for the Deal

In order to determine who acts as the designated dealer at the start of a new game, the house dealer shuffles the cards and deals one card face-up to each player at the table. The player with the highest card is the designated dealer. In the event of a tie, the highest suit takes precedence in the following order from highest to lowest: spades, hearts, diamonds, clubs. An alternative rule is to disregard the suits and declare the person dealt the first ace the high-card winner.

The Play of Poker

Selecting a Game

Most poker games fall under one of three types: Community Card Poker, Draw Poker and Stud Poker. While all three types can be found in various cardrooms, community card poker has become the dominating force in poker over the last few years.

Community Card Poker

Players are dealt cards face-down which they must use in conjunction with community cards dealt face-up. The community cards are placed in the middle of the table to be shared by all players to make their best poker hand. Community card games accommodate more players at a table than both draw and stud games, making it well-suited for tournaments with large player fields. Texas Hold 'Em and Omaha are the two most popular forms of community card poker. Texas Hold 'Em is the game of choice in most cardrooms largely due to televised tournaments that have educated people on the game. It is currently the game played at the main event of the World Series of Poker to determine the world champion.

Draw Poker

Players receive cards face-down which they may replace with cards from the deck to improve their hand. Due to its simplicity, draw poker is the first type of poker most people learn how to play. With only two standard betting rounds and a maximum of seven players per table, draw is not found in many cardrooms today, but remains a home game favorite. Lowball, where the lowest hand wins, is the only form of draw poker found at the World Series of Poker.

Stud Poker

Players receive a combination of downcards and upcards that they use to make their best poker hand. Stud poker has multiple betting rounds and is played typically with a maximum of seven players per table. This type of poker requires a great deal of concentration as players must pay attention to other player's upcards and remember cards that have been folded in order to strategize. This type of poker is a non-positional game, which means the first player to act may change on each betting round based on the exposed cards. Seven-Card Stud is the most popular form of stud poker and is played in most cardrooms as well as at the World Series of Poker.

Selecting a Betting Structure

Once the type of game is selected the betting structure of the game must be established. There are three common types of betting structures: Limit (including fixed-limit and spread-limit), Pot-Limit and No-Limit.

Fixed-Limit

Players in a fixed-limit poker game, commonly referred to as limit, must bet in structured increments on each round of betting. Each raise must equal the same betting increment. For example, in a 10/20 limit game Player A bets $10 on the first round of betting, Player B raises to $20, Player C raises to $30. Players may continue to raise the bet in the same increment until the maximum number of raises is met. Most limit games allow a bet and a maximum of three or four raises. The betting amount changes based on the round of betting in a limit game. On the higher limit betting rounds in the same 10/20 game, if Player A bet, the amount would be $20, Player B would have to raise the bet to $40, and Player C would have to raise to $60. In heads-up play, the maximum number of bets is often removed and players may make an unlimited number of raises. Rules on the maximum number of raises permitted, including heads-up play, should be included in every cardroom rulebook.

The following explains common betting patterns in fixed-limit poker games:

Community Card Poker

On the first two rounds of betting (before and after the flop) the betting amount is the lower of the stated limits. The limited bet doubles on the last two rounds of betting (the turn and river cards). A bet and a maximum of three raises are typically permitted on each round of betting.

Draw Poker

The betting amount is often the lower limit on the early betting round and the higher limit on the last round of betting. Usually one bet and a maximum of three or four raises are permitted.

Stud Poker

The betting amount is the lower limit on the first two rounds except when there is an open pair on the second round of betting (the second upcard) at which time any player is permitted to bet the lower or the higher limit. For example, in a 5/10 limit game with an open pair on the second round of betting, the high-hand player may bet either $5 or $10. If he bets $5, other players may call $5, raise $5 (making the bet $10) or raise $10 (making the bet $15). If a player chooses to raise $10, which is the higher limit, all other players wishing to raise, must raise in increments of $10.

The betting amount is always the higher limit on the last three rounds of betting. On each round of betting a bet and a maximum of three raises are typically permitted. Completion of the bring-in bet does not constitute a raise.

Spread-Limit

Spread-limit is a flexible form of limit poker where players may bet within a specified range. For example, in a 5/20 spread-limit game, players may bet anywhere from $5 to $20 on any round of betting. Bets and raises in a spread-limit game are usually required to match or exceed the increment of the previous bet up to the higher of the stated limits. For example, in a 5/20 spread-limit game if a player bets $6, the next player may fold, call the $6 bet or raise the bet to a minimum of $12 and a maximum of $26 ($6 call + $20 raise).

Another form of a spread-limit game entails raising the betting range on later rounds of betting. For example in a 5/10, 10/20 spread-limit game, players may bet any amount from $5 to $10 on early betting rounds and any amount from $10 to $20 on later betting rounds. Spread-limit games are found more commonly in home games than casinos.

Pot-Limit

Players in a pot-limit game may make a bet up to the amount of money in the pot on any round of betting. Players wishing to raise must bet a minimum amount of the last bet or raise. If no bet has been made the first bet is equal to the amount of the antes or the blinds. The small blind is usually rounded up to the size of the big blind when calculating the size of the pot in games using blinds. When calculating the amount a player can raise in pot-limit, first the call is added to the present pot, then the player may raise the amount in the pot. There is typically no limit to the number of raises allowed in a pot-limit game.

An example of betting in pot-limit poker is as follows:

> The pot contains $50 and Player A bets $25, Player B may fold, call the $25 or raise up to $100 more making the pot total $200 ($50 pot + $25 bet + $25 call from raiser + the $100 raise). Player C may then fold, call the $125 ($25 bet + $100 raise), or reraise an amount from $100 more (Player B's raise) up to $325 more, making the total wager $425.

No-Limit

Players in a no-limit game may bet all of the money or chips in front of them on any round of betting. This type of game is well suited for games with four or fewer betting rounds and therefore is common to community card and draw poker. Games with more than four betting rounds, such as Seven-Card Stud, are typically played using fixed-limits.

The opening bet in a game using antes must be at least double the ante amount. In a game using blinds, the first raise must be at least double the amount of the big blind. Players wishing to raise in a no-limit game must bet a minimum amount of the last bet or raise and a maximum amount that is the amount the player has at the table. There is typically no limit to the number of raises allowed in a no-limit game.

An example of betting in a no-limit community card or draw poker game using blinds is as follows:

> The pot contains $15 which includes a $5 small blind and a $10 big blind. Player A calls the $10, making the pot $25. Player B raises to $60 ($10 call + $50 bet), making the pot $85. Player C may then fold, call the $60, or reraise at least $50 more up to any amount he has in front of him.

The Shuffle

The dealer will typically mix the cards face-down in the center of the table prior to the first deal or whenever a new deck is introduced. This process is known as "scrambling" and will be done at any time during the game at the dealer's discretion or upon request by a player. This process is added assurance that the cards are being adequately mixed. After the scramble, the cards are gathered, arranged, and riffled three or four times. The dealer will then "cut the deck" by separating it in half and placing the top half on a cut card and the bottom half on top.

Several casinos have shuffling machines built into their poker tables. The machine is designed to randomly shuffle the cards for the dealer. This eases the work of the dealer and reduces the risk of inefficient manual shuffling. The dealer simply presses a button to open the machine, retrieves the deck of cards and places the previous deck in the machine to be shuffled. The dealer then cuts the cards and proceeds to deal.

Shuffling without a House Dealer

The duty of shuffling the cards is shared by other players at the table when a house dealer is not provided, such as in a home game. The following explains an expedient process commonly used for shuffling cards in a game without a house dealer:

1. Player A offers the player to his left the option to cut the first deck of cards. He then deals each player a hand. He gathers the cards when the hand is complete and begins shuffling
2. Player B offers the player to her left the option to cut a second deck cards. She then deals each player a hand with the second deck of cards while Player A finishes shuffling the first deck
3. Player A passes the first deck of shuffled cards to Player C seated two places to his left
4. Player B gathers the cards when the second hand is complete and the process continues around the table

Stimulating Action

In order to stimulate action in a poker game it is common for players to post an ante or a blind prior to dealing each hand. Some games also require players to make a forced bet known as a bring-in bet after the deal. This money creates a starting pot for which the players compete.

Antes

In games that use antes, every player must post a small, predetermined bet amount into the pot prior to the start of each hand. All players contribute to the pot at the start of every hand. Antes are commonly used for games such as draw poker and any type of dealer's choice game that change from one variant game to another throughout the course of play. Antes are sometimes used in addition to blinds and bring-in bets.

Blinds

In blind games, the first player to the left of the dealer must post a blind bet half the size of the minimum bet, called the small blind. The second player to the left of the dealer posts a blind bet the size of the minimum bet, called the big blind. After each hand is complete and the dealer position changes, the blinds are posted by the next players seated one and two seats to the left of the dealer and continue around the table. Blinds are commonly used in community-card and lowball games.

Bring-In Bets

Bring-in bets are forced bets used in stud games in addition to an ante. It is a percentage of a full bet that must be made on the first betting round by the player dealt the highest or lowest upcard, depending on the variant of stud poker being played.

The Deal

The dealer deals cards one at a time to each player starting with the player to the left of the designated dealer and continuing clockwise around the table until each player has the appropriate number of cards.

Action

Action is when a player checks, calls, bets, raises or folds in a poker hand. Players should make every effort to clarify their intended action in order to avoid any misunderstandings that could lead to conflict or disruption of the game. Verbal actions are helpful to the dealer as well as the players, but it should be clear in the cardroom rulebook whether or not all verbal declarations are binding. For example, in a game where verbal declarations are binding, if a player faced with a bet says, "Call," that player must match the betting amount and cannot proceed with any other action.

The following actions are the options repeated on each round of betting for active players in a poker hand:

Bet

To make a wager.

The first bet made in a game using antes is called the opening bet. Each player, starting with the player to the left of the dealer may make a wager into the pot that other players must call, fold to, or raise. Some games require players to have at least a pair of jacks or better to make this first bet. On every betting round thereafter the first active player may make a voluntary bet that other players must call, fold to, or raise.

In a game using blinds, the first bet is the mandatory bets made by the players seated in the first two seats to the left of the dealer. The first player to act may either call the large blind bet, fold or raise the blind bet. On every betting round thereafter the first active player may make a voluntary bet that other players must call, fold to, or raise.

In a stud game the first bet is the forced bring-in bet which other players must call, fold to, or raise. On every betting round thereafter the first active player may make a voluntary bet that other players must call, fold to, or raise.

Call

To match the betting amount after a player has made a bet.

A player may verbally state, "Call," or place the appropriate amount of chips out front and say nothing.

Raise

To increase the bet.

Once a bet has been made, another player may match the bet and raise an additional amount that other players must call, fold to, or reraise up to the number of raises allowed. A player may verbally state, "Raise," or place a bet no less than double the amount of the previous bet out front. If a player places an oversized chip into the pot without saying, "Raise," most cardrooms will consider the action a call.

Check

To pass the option to bet, yet remain active in the hand.

Checking is only permitted when a player is not faced with a bet. A player may verbally state, "Check," or rap the table with his or her hand.

Check-Raise

To check initially, then raise if another player bets on the same betting round.

This action is often used as a tactic for slow-playing a big poker hand in order to trap an opponent into betting. A small number of games do not permit check-raising. It should be clearly stated in the rulebook if check-raising is not allowed.

Fold

To discard a hand and concede the pot.

Players faced with a bet may fold their hand by verbally stating, "Fold," or by pushing their cards to the dealer. In stud-type games, players will sometimes turn all of their upcards face-down to indicate a fold. When cards are folded they are surrendered into a discard pile known as the "muck." In home games the muck is often near the pot. In cardrooms, the muck is kept close to the dealer.

Declaring

The actions of checking, calling, betting, raising and folding are common to every form of poker. There is a less common action used primarily in home games: declaring. Declaring is done at certain intervals during a hand, usually right before a betting round occurs. It can pertain to staying or folding in a hand as well as declaring a high or low value of a hand.

The following are two common methods of declaring:

1-2-3 Drop

This form of declaring is usually done at the beginning of a hand when players are forced to decide whether they wish to play or fold a hand. Players hold their downcards at an arms length toward the center of the table. The designated dealer states, "1-2-3 drop," and players simultaneously drop their cards if they wish to fold and hold on to their cards if they wish to stay in the hand.

Chips in the Hand

This form of declaring is often done in place of the "1-2-3 Drop" method. Players secretly place one or two chips in their hand then simultaneously reveal them. One chip indicates the player wishes to fold and two indicates the player wishes to stay in the hand. This method of declaring with chips is also commonly used to declare in a high-low split pot game. Players place one, two or three chips in their hand. One chip indicates the player is contending for the highest hand, two chips indicates the player is contending for the lowest hand, and three chips indicates the player is contending for both the highest and lowest hand.

Uncontested Pot

When all but one hand has been folded, the remaining player wins the pot without any need to show the winning hand except in cases where the player must prove required conditions were met, such as in Jacks or Better Draw Poker.

Showdown

Players must turn their cards face-up at the end of the hand in order to be eligible to win a contested pot. This is called the showdown. Once the cards are face-up, the dealer determines the best poker hand and declares the winning hand. The dealer will kill all losing hands and push the pot to the winner. In a community card game, the dealer pushes forward the community cards used to make the best hand for clarity. A player who contests the dealer's decision must do so at this time or concede the pot.

Pushing the Pot

The dealer is responsible for making sure that all bets are in the pot once the winning hand has been announced. The dealer should then push the chips to the player with the winning hand, gather the cards and begin the dealing process for the next hand.

Split Pots

When two or more players have the winning hand, the dealer must divide the pot into equal amounts and pay each winning player the exact amount. This occurs with tied hands and in high-low split games where the highest and the lowest poker hand split the pot.

The Odd Chip

When the pot amount is not exactly even, the dealer must make change to distribute the correct amount. If an odd chip of the lowest denomination still remains, the house must decide how to distribute the chip. The following three methods are most common: 1) The winning player first to the left of the designated dealer receives the extra chip. 2) The player with the highest card by suit receives the extra chip in high games and the lowest card by suit receives it in low games. 3) In high-low split games, it is common for the high hand winner to receive the extra chip. The method used should be stated in the cardroom rules.

Quartering the Pot

In high-low split games it is sometimes necessary to split the pot between the highest and lowest hand and split the low half of the pot again when two players hold the same low hand, this is called "Getting Quartered."

Side Pots

When more than two players are involved in a hand and one player does not have enough chips to call an entire bet, a side pot is created. The dealer will pull an equal amount of chips from each player into the main pot. Once a player has less than the amount needed to call an entire bet, the dealer will create a secondary pot that only the players with additional chips are eligible to win. The players with additional chips may continue to bet one another and contend for both the main pot and the side pot. If another player runs out of chips while the betting continues, the dealer will create a second side pot of which only the players with additional chips will be eligible to win. An additional side pot will be created each time a player runs out of money throughout the duration of a hand.

At the point of showdown the dealer will ask players to reveal their hands in a specific order. The players contending for a side pot will show hands first, followed by the player(s) contending for the main pot. If more than one side pot exists, the dealer will ask the players to reveal hands starting with the players involved in the last side pot created.

Bad Beat Jackpots

A bad beat jackpot is a progressive prize pool offered by some cardrooms or online poker websites when an extremely good hand is beaten by an exceptional hand. The money is accrued from an additional rake taken out of each hand for each game that participates in a bad beat jackpot. Most bad beat jackpots have minimum qualifiers and are offered typically in Texas Hold 'Em, Omaha, and Seven-Card Stud. A common qualifier in Texas Hold 'Em is that a full house of aces full of queens or better must be beat and players must use both of their downcards to make their five-card poker hand. In both Omaha and Seven-Card Stud, usually four-of-a-kind or better must be beat in order to qualify for the bad beat jackpot. The jackpot is typically distributed in the following manner: 50% is paid to the player with the losing hand, 25% is paid to the player with the winning hand, and the remaining 25% is divided among the players dealt into the hand.

Leaving

Leaving the Game

Players may leave a live game at any time. It is appropriate to place chips in a chip rack and proceed to the cashier cage to exchange them for money. In home games, after placing chips in the rack, players typically announce to the dealer or houseperson that they would like to "cash in." The houseperson will verify the chip count and pay the player the appropriate amount.

Poker Tournaments

Tournaments

A tournament structure involves people buying in for a set amount of money in exchange for chips. All players are issued an equal number of chips. The players play poker with these chips until they lose all of their chips and are eliminated from the tournament. The last player with chips remaining at the table is declared the tournament winner. Tournaments have different formats and prize awards, which should be published and available at the time of buy-in. Directors hosting a cash prize tournament wait until all players are registered before announcing the exact distribution of the prize pool. The Poker Tournament Directors Association rules and the World Series of Poker player rules are included in Chapter Two.

Seating Positions in a Tournament

Seats are assigned for players in a tournament. For large tournaments, such as World Series of Poker and World Poker Tour events, a computer randomly generates assigned seats as players register for a tournament. For small tournaments, such as single table satellites and home game tournaments, seats are typically assigned by cards. The dealer pulls an equal number of cards for each player, shuffles them and places them face-down in the center of the table. Each player selects a card and sits in the seat number based on the hand ranking of the card. For example, the player that selects the 8♣, sits in the eight seat.

For multi-table tournaments, the dealer pulls an equal number of cards of each suit and assigns each table to a suit. The following example explains this process:

A. Thirty players have paid to enter the tournament
B. The dealer, tournament director or host assigns table one clubs, table two hearts and table three spades
C. The dealer pulls club-suited cards Ace–10, heart-suited cards Ace–10 and spade-suited cards Ace–10 from the deck
D. The dealer scrambles the thirty cards face-down in the center of the table
E. Players select a card and proceed to the table and seat number that corresponds to the card. For example, the player that selected the 8♣ would sit at table one, seat eight

Tipping the Tournament Dealer

It is customary for the winning player(s) to give an employed dealer a tip, usually a small percentage of the prize pool, after the tournament is over and prize money has been distributed. It is appropriate to subtract the buy-in amount from the prize pool total when calculating the percentage. In large tournaments with multiple dealers, it is proper to give the dealer tip to the tournament director and ask that the money be distributed amongst the tournament dealers.

CHAPTER TWO

PROFESSIONAL POKER RULES

The following sets of rules were written by poker industry professionals for major cardrooms, casinos, and poker tournaments. These rules govern the particulars of each establishment and or organization hosting a poker game. These rules do not cover the basics of poker which are covered in Chapter One.

Professional poker players play in several different games, often traveling to tournaments and cardrooms in different locations. While cardroom rules change from one location to another, due to differing laws and local customs, players expect a certain degree of standardization when it comes to poker rules. This chapter provides that information in the four most widely used sets of cardroom rules: Robert's Rules of Poker for Casinos, Robert's Rules of Poker for Private Games, Poker Tournament Directors Association rules, and the World Series of Poker player rules.

Future editions of *The Game Day Poker Almanac Official Rules of Poker* will include updated versions of these professional poker rules.

ROBERT'S RULES OF POKER

Version 10

Reprinted courtesy of Bob Ciaffone

"Robert's Rules of Poker" is authored by Robert Ciaffone, better known in the poker world as Bob Ciaffone, a leading authority on cardroom rules. He is the person who has selected which rules to use, and formatted, organized, and worded the text. Nearly all these rules are substantively in common use for poker, but many improved ideas for wording and organization are employed throughout this work. A lot of the rules are similar to those used in the rulebook of cardrooms where he has acted as a rules consultant and rules drafter. Ciaffone authored the rulebook for the Poker Players Association (founded in 1984, now defunct), the first comprehensive set of poker rules for the general public. He has done extensive work on rules for the Las Vegas Hilton, The Mirage, and Hollywood Park Casino, and assisted many other cardrooms. Ciaffone is a regular columnist for Card Player magazine, and can be reached through that publication. This rulebook will be periodically revised, so suggestions are welcome at www.pokercoach.com.

Poker rules are widely used and freely copied, so it is impossible to construct a rulebook without using many rules that exist as part of a rule set of some cardroom. If such a rule is used, no credit is given to the source (which is unlikely to be the original one for the rule).

The goal of this rulebook is to produce the best set of rules in existence, and make it generally available, so any person or cardroom can use it who so desires. The purpose is the betterment of poker.

The general philosophy used in this rulebook is to make the rules sufficiently detailed so a decision-maker will know what the proper ruling is in each situation. A rule should do more than produce the right ruling. It should be stated so the decision-maker can refer to specific language in the rulebook, to have the ruling accepted as correct.

The author has strongly supported uniform poker rules, and applauds the work done in this direction by the Poker Tournament Directors Association (TDA). Nearly all the rules herein are compatible with the TDA rules, although there are some slight differences in wording.

TABLE OF CONTENTS

1.0: PROPER BEHAVIOR

1.1: CONDUCT CODE

Management will attempt to maintain a pleasant environment for all our customers and employees, but is not responsible for the conduct of any player. We have established a code of conduct, and may deny the use of our cardroom to violators. The following are not permitted:

1. Collusion with another player or any other form of cheating.
2. Verbally or physically threatening any patron or employee.
3. Using profanity or obscene language.
4. Creating a disturbance by arguing, shouting or making excessive noise.
5. Throwing, tearing, bending or crumpling cards.
6. Destroying or defacing property.
7. Using an illegal substance.
8. Carrying a weapon.

1.2: POKER ETIQUETTE

The following actions are improper, and grounds for warning, suspending or barring a violator:

1. Deliberately acting out of turn.
2. Deliberately splashing chips into the pot.
3. Agreeing to check a hand out when a third player is all-in.
4. Reading a hand for another player at the showdown before it has been placed face-up on the table.
5. Telling anyone to turn a hand face-up at the showdown.
6. Revealing the contents of a live hand in a multihanded pot before the betting is complete.
7. Revealing the contents of a folded hand before the betting is complete. Do not divulge the contents of a hand during a deal even to someone not in the pot, so you do not leave any possibility of the information being transmitted to an active player.
8. Needlessly stalling the action of a game.
9. Deliberately discarding hands away from the muck. Cards should be released in a low line of flight, at a moderate rate of speed (not at the dealer's hands or chip-rack).
10. Stacking chips in a manner that interferes with dealing or viewing cards.
11. Making statements or taking action that could unfairly influence the course of play, whether or not the offender is involved in the pot.
12. Using a cell phone at the table.

1.3: TOBACCO USE

(These rules are for an establishment that does not completely bar smoking.)

1. The seat on each side of the dealer is a nonsmoking seat.
2. Cigar or pipe smoking is not allowed in the cardroom.
3. Smoking by a guest or spectator is not allowed.

2.0: HOUSE POLICIES

2.1: DECISION-MAKING

1. Management reserves the right to make decisions in the spirit of fairness, even if a strict interpretation of the rules may indicate a different ruling.
2. Decisions of the shift supervisor are final.
3. The proper time to draw attention to a mistake is when it occurs or is first noticed. Any delay may affect the ruling.
4. If an incorrect rule interpretation or decision by an employee is made in good faith, the establishment has no liability.
5. A ruling may be made regarding a pot if it has been requested before the next deal starts (or before the game either ends or changes to another table). Otherwise, the result of a deal must stand. The first riffle of the shuffle marks the start for a deal.
6. If a pot has been incorrectly awarded and mingled with chips that were not in the pot, and the time limit for a ruling request given in the previous rule has been observed, management may determine how much was in the pot by reconstructing the betting, and then transfer that amount to the proper player.
7. To keep the action moving, it is possible that a game may be asked to continue even though a decision is delayed. The delay could be to check the overhead camera tape, get the shift supervisor to give the ruling, or for some other good reason. In such circumstances, a pot or portion of it may be impounded by the house while the decision is pending.
8. The same action may have a different meaning, depending on who does it, so the possible intent of an offender will be taken into

consideration. Some factors here are the person's amount of poker experience and past record.

9. A player, before he acts, is entitled to request and receive information as to whether any opposing hand is alive or dead, or whether a wager is of sufficient size to reopen the betting.

2.2: PROCEDURES

1. Only one person may play a hand.
2. No one is allowed to play another player's chips.
3. Management will decide when to start or close any game.
4. Collections (seat rental fees) are paid in advance. In all time-collection games, the dealer is required to pick up the collection from each player before dealing. A player not wishing to pay collection may play one courtesy hand in stud, and may play until the blind in button games, provided no one is waiting for the game. If there is more than one person on the list for that game when the collection becomes due, everyone must pay collection. A new player is not required to pay if there is either no list or only one person waiting.
5. Cash is not allowed on the table. All cash should be changed into chips in order to play. If a player seems unaware of this rule and tries to play unnoticed cash that was on the table during a pot, the dealer may let the cash play if no one in the pot objects, then have all the cash changed into chips after the hand. Any chips from another cardroom are not permitted on the table, do not play in the game, and when found will be treated similarly to unnoticed cash. [See 16.0: Explanations, discussion #5, for more information on this rule.]
6. Money and chips may be removed for security purposes when leaving the table. The establishment is not responsible for any shortage or removal of chips left on the table during a player's absence, even though we will try to protect everyone as best we can. All removed funds must be fully restored when returning to the game.
7. If you return to the same game within one hour of cashing out, your buy-in must be equal to the amount removed when leaving that game.
8. All games are table stakes (except "playing behind" as given in the next rule). Only the chips in front of a player at the start of a deal may play for that hand, except for chips not yet received that a player has purchased. The amount bought must be announced to the table, or only the amount of the minimum buy-in plays. Awareness

of the amount being in play for each opponent is an important part of poker. All chips and money must be kept in plain view.

9. "Playing behind" is allowed only for the amount of purchased chips while awaiting their arrival. The amount in play must be announced to the table, or only the amount of the minimum buy-in plays.

10. Playing out of a rack is not allowed.

11. Permission is required before taking a seat in a game.

12. Playing over without permission from the floorperson is not allowed. A playover box is required. Permission from the absent player is not necessary.

13. Pushing bets ("saving" or "potting out") is not allowed.

14. Pushing an ante or posting for another person is not allowed.

15. Splitting pots will not be allowed in any game. Chopping the big and small blind by taking them back when all other players have folded is allowed in button games.

16. Insurance propositions are not allowed. Dealing twice (or three times) when all-in is permitted at big-bet poker.

17. The game's betting limit will not be changed if two or more players object. Raising the limit is subject to management approval.

18. Players must keep their cards in full view. This means above table-level and not past the edge of the table. The cards should not be covered by the hands in a manner to completely conceal them.

19. Any player is entitled to a clear view of an opponent's chips. Higher denomination chips should be easily visible.

20. Your chips may be picked up if you are away from the table for more than 30 minutes. Your absence may be extended if you notify a floorperson in advance. Frequent or continuous absences may cause your chips to be picked up from the table.

21. A lock-up in a new game will be picked up after five minutes if someone is waiting to play. No seat may be locked up for more than ten minutes if someone is waiting to play.

22. A new deck must be used for at least a full round (once around the table) before it may be changed, and a new setup must be used for at least an hour, unless a deck is defective or damaged, or cards become sticky.

23. Looking through the discards or deck stub is not allowed.

24. After a deal ends, dealers are asked to not show what card would have been dealt.

25. A player is expected to pay attention to the game and not hold up play. Activity that interferes with this such as reading at the table is discouraged, and the player will be asked to cease if a problem is caused.
26. A non-player may not sit at the table.
27. In non-tournament games, you may have a guest sit behind you if no one in the game objects. It is improper for a guest to look at any hand other then your own.
28. Speaking a foreign language during a deal is not allowed.

2.3: SEATING

1. You must be present to add your name to a waiting list.
2. It is the player's responsibility to be in the playing area and hear the list being called. A player who intends to leave the playing area should notify the list-person, and can leave money for a lockup. The lockup amount is $20.
3. When there is more than one game of the same stakes and poker form, and a must-move is not being used, the house will control the seating of new players to best preserve the viability of existing games. A new player will be sent to the game most in need of an additional player. A transfer to a similar game is not allowed if the game being left will then have fewer players than the game being entered.
4. A player may not hold a seat in more than one game.
5. The house reserves the right to require that any two players not play in the same game (husband and wife, relatives, business partners, and so forth).
6. When a button game starts, active players will draw a card for the button position. The button will be awarded to the highest card by suit for all high and high-low games, and to the lowest card by suit for all low games.
7. To avoid a seating dispute, a supervisor may decide to start the game with one extra player over the normal number. If so, a seat will be removed as soon as someone quits the game.
8. In a new game, the player who arrives at the table the earliest gets first choice of remaining seats. If two players want the same seat and arrive at the same time, the higher player on the list has preference. A player playing a pot in another game may have a designated seat locked up until that hand is finished. Management may reserve a

certain seat for a player for a good reason, such as to assist reading the board for a person with a vision problem.

9. To protect an existing game, a forced move may be invoked when an additional game of the same type and limit is started. The must-move list is maintained in the same order as the original waiting list. If a player refuses to move into the main game, that player will be forced to quit, and cannot play in the must-move game or get on that list for one hour.

10. In all button games, a player going from a must-move game to the main game may play until due for the big blind. The player must then enter the game as a new player, and may either post an amount equal to the big blind or wait for the big blind. In all stud games, a player may play only one more hand before moving.

11. You must play in a new game or must-move game to retain your place on the list, if with your playing there would be three or fewer empty seats.

12. A player who is already in the game has precedence over a new player for any seat when it becomes available. However, no change will occur after a new player has been seated, or after that player's buy-in or marker has been placed on the table, unless that particular seat had been previously requested. For players already in the game, the one who asks the earliest has preference for a seat change.

13. In all button games, a player voluntarily locking up a seat in another game must move immediately if there is a waiting list of two or more names for the seat being vacated, except that the player is entitled to play the button if a blind has already been taken. Otherwise, a player may play up to the blind before moving. In a stud game, a player changing tables may play only the present hand if someone is waiting for the seat being vacated, or one more hand when no one is waiting.

14. When a game breaks, each player may draw a card to determine the seating order for a similar game. The floorperson draws a card for an absent player. If the card entitles the absent player to an immediate seat, the player has until due for the big blind in a button game to take the seat (two hands in a stud game), and will be put first up on the list if not back in time.

3.0: GENERAL POKER RULES

3.1 THE BUY-IN

1. When you enter a game, you must make a full buy-in. At limit poker, a full buy-in is at least ten times the maximum bet for the game being played, unless designated otherwise.
2. You are allowed to make only one short buy-in for a game. Adding to your stack is not considered a buy-in, and may be done in any quantity between hands.
3. A player coming from a broken game or must-move game to a game of the same limit may continue to play the same amount of money, even if it is less than the minimum buy-in. A player switching games voluntarily must have the proper buy-in size for the new game. A player switching games is not required to buy in for any more than the minimum amount.

3.2 MISDEALS

1. Once action begins, a misdeal cannot be called. The deal will be played, and no money will be returned to any player whose hand is fouled. In button games, action is considered to occur when two players after the blinds have acted on their hands. In stud games, action is considered to occur when two players after the forced bet have acted on their hands.
2. The following circumstances cause a misdeal, provided attention is called to the error before two players have acted on their hands.
    (a) The first or second card of the hand has been exposed by a dealer error.
    (b) Two or more cards have been exposed by the dealer.
    (c) Two or more boxed cards (improperly faced cards) are found.
    (d) Two or more extra cards have been dealt in the starting hands of a game.
    (e) An incorrect number of cards has been dealt to a player, except the top card may be dealt if it goes to the player in proper sequence.
    (f) Any card has been dealt out of the proper sequence (except an exposed card may be replaced by the burncard).
    (g) The button was out of position.

(h) The first card was dealt to the wrong position.

(i) Cards have been dealt to an empty seat or a player not entitled to a hand.

(j) A player has been dealt out who is entitled to a hand. This player must be present at the table or have posted a blind or ante.

3.3: DEAD HANDS

1. Your hand is declared dead if:

   (a) You fold or announce that you are folding when facing a bet or a raise.

   (b) You throw your hand away in a forward motion causing another player to act behind you (even if not facing a bet).

   (c) In stud, when facing a bet, you pick your upcards off the table, turn your upcards face-down, or mix your upcards and downcards together.

   (d) The hand does not contain the proper number of cards for that particular game (except at stud a hand missing the final card may be ruled live, and at lowball and draw high a hand with too few cards before the draw is live). [See 16.0: Explanations, discussion #4, for more information on the stud portion of this rule.]

   (e) You act on a hand with a joker as a holecard in a game not using a joker. (A player who acts on a hand without looking at a card assumes the liability of finding an improper card, as given in 3.4: Irregularities, rule #8.)

   (f) You have the clock on you when facing a bet or raise and exceed the specified time limit.

2. Cards thrown into the muck may be ruled dead. However, a hand that is clearly identifiable may be retrieved and ruled live at management's discretion if doing so is in the best interest of the game. An extra effort should be made to rule a hand retrievable if it was folded as a result of incorrect information given to the player.

3. Cards thrown into another player's hand are dead, whether they are face-up or face-down.

3.4: IRREGULARITIES

1. In button games, if it is discovered that the button was placed incorrectly on the previous hand, the button and blinds will be corrected for the new hand in a manner that gives every player one chance for each position on the round (if possible).

2. You must protect your own hand at all times. Your cards may be protected with your hands, a chip or other object placed on top of them. If you fail to protect your hand, you will have no redress if it becomes fouled or the dealer accidentally kills it.

3. If a card with a different color back appears during a hand, all action is void and all chips in the pot are returned to the respective bettors. If a card with a different color back is discovered in the stub, all action stands.

4. If two cards of the same rank and suit are found, all action is void, and all chips in the pot are returned to the players who wagered them (subject to next rule).

5. A player who knows the deck is defective has an obligation to point this out. If such a player instead tries to win a pot by taking aggressive action (trying for a freeroll), the player may lose the right to a refund, and the chips may be required to stay in the pot for the next deal.

6. If there is extra money in the pot on a deal as a result of forfeited money from the previous deal (as per rule #5), or some similar reason, only a player dealt in on the previous deal is entitled to a hand.

7. A card discovered face-up in the deck (boxed card) will be treated as a meaningless scrap of paper. A card being treated as a scrap of paper will be replaced by the next card below it in the deck, except when the next card has already been dealt face-down to another player and mixed in with other downcards. In that case, the card that was face-up in the deck will be replaced after all other cards are dealt for that round.

8. A joker that appears in a game where it is not used is treated as a scrap of paper. Discovery of a joker does not cause a misdeal. If the joker is discovered before a player acts on his or her hand, it is replaced as in the previous rule. If the player does not call attention to the joker before acting, then the player has a dead hand.

9. If you play a hand without looking at all of your cards, you assume the liability of having an irregular card or an improper joker.

10. One or more cards missing from the deck does not invalidate the results of a hand.

11. Before the first round of betting, if a dealer deals one additional card, it is returned to the deck and used as the burncard.

12. Procedure for an exposed card varies with the poker form, and is given in the section for each game. A card that is flashed by a dealer is treated as an exposed card. A card that is flashed by a player will play. To obtain a ruling on whether a card was exposed and should be replaced, a player should announce that the card was flashed or exposed before looking at it. A downcard dealt off the table is an exposed card.

13. If a card is exposed due to dealer error, a player does not have an option to take or reject the card. The situation will be governed by the rules for the particular game being played.

14. If you drop any cards out of your hand onto the floor, you must still play them.

15. If the dealer prematurely deals any cards before the betting is complete, those cards will not play, even if a player who has not acted decides to fold.

16. If the dealer fails to burn a card or burns more than one card, the error should be corrected if discovered before betting action has started for that round. Once action has been taken on a boardcard, the card must stand. Whether the error is able to be corrected or not, subsequent cards dealt should be those that would have come if no error had occurred. For example, if two cards were burned, one of the cards should be put back on the deck and used for the burncard on the next round. On the last round, if there was no betting because a player was all-in, the error should be corrected if discovered before the pot has been awarded, provided the deck stub, boardcards and burncards are all sufficiently intact to determine the proper replacement card.

17. If the deck stub gets fouled for some reason, such as the dealer believing the deal is over and dropping the deck, the deal must still be played out, and the deck reconstituted in as fair a way as possible.

3.5: BETTING AND RAISING

1. The smallest chip that may be wagered in a game is the smallest chip used in the antes, blinds, rake or collection. (Certain games may use a special rule that does not allow chips used only in house revenue to play.) Smaller chips than this do not play even in quantity, so a player wanting action on such chips must change them up between deals. If betting is in dollar units or greater, a fraction of a dollar does not play. A player going all-in must put all chips that play into the pot.

2. Check-raise is permitted in all games, except in certain forms of lowball.

3. In no-limit and pot-limit games, unlimited raising is allowed.

4. In limit poker, for a pot involving three or more players who are not all-in, these limits on raises apply:
    (a) A game with three or more betting rounds allows a maximum of a bet and three raises.
    (b) A game with two betting rounds (such as lowball or draw) allows a maximum of a bet and four raises. [See 16.0: Explanations, discussion #6, for more information on this rule.]

5. Unlimited raising is allowed in heads-up play except in tournaments. This applies any time the action becomes heads-up before the raising has been capped. Once the raising is capped on a betting round, it cannot be uncapped by a subsequent fold that leaves two players heads-up. (For tournament play in limit events there will be a limit to raises even when heads-up until the tournament is down to two players.)

6. Any wager not all-in must be at least the size of the previous bet or raise in that round.

7. In limit play, an all-in wager of less than half a bet does not reopen the betting for any player who has already acted and is in the pot for all previous bets. A player who has not yet acted (or had the betting reopened to him by another player's action), facing an all-in wager of less than half a bet, may fold, call or complete the wager. An all-in wager of a half a bet or more is treated as a full bet, and a player may fold, call or make a full raise. (An example of a full raise on a $20 betting round is raising a $15 all-in bet to $35.) Multiple all-in wagers, each of an amount too small to individually qualify

as a raise, still act as a raise and reopen the betting if the resulting wager size to a player qualifies as a raise.

8. In limit poker, if you make a forward motion with chips and thus cause another player to act, you may be forced to complete your action.

9. A verbal statement in turn denotes your action, is binding, and takes precedence over a differing physical action.

10. Rapping the table with your hand is a pass.

11. Deliberately acting out of turn will not be tolerated. A player who checks out of turn may not bet or raise on the next turn to act. A player who has called out of turn may not change his wager to a raise on the next turn to act. An action or verbal declaration out of turn is binding unless the action to that player is subsequently changed by a bet or raise. If there is an intervening call, an action may be ruled binding.

12. To retain the right to act, a player must stop the action by calling "time" (or an equivalent word). Failure to stop the action before three or more players have acted behind you may cause you to lose the right to act. You cannot forfeit your right to act if any player in front of you has not acted, only if you fail to act when it legally becomes your turn. Therefore, if you wait for someone whose turn comes before you, and three or more players act behind you, this still does not hinder your right to act.

13. A player who bets or calls by releasing chips into the pot is bound by that action and must make the amount of the wager correct. (This also applies right before the showdown when putting chips into the pot causes the opponent to show the winning hand before the full amount needed to call has been put into the pot.) However, if you are unaware that the pot has been raised, you may withdraw that money and reconsider your action, provided that no one else has acted after you. At pot-limit or no-limit betting, if there is a gross misunderstanding concerning the amount of the wager, see 14.0: No-Limit and Pot-Limit, Rule 8.

14. String raises are not allowed. The dealer should enforce obvious infractions to this string-raise law without being asked. To protect your right to raise, you should either declare your intention verbally or place the proper amount of chips into the pot. Putting a full bet plus a half-bet or more into the pot is considered to be the same as

announcing a raise, and the raise must be completed. (This does not apply in the use of a single chip of greater value.)

15. If you put a single chip in the pot that is larger than the bet, but do not announce a raise, you are assumed to have only called. Example: In a $3-$6 game, when a player bets $6 and the next player puts a $25 chip in the pot without saying anything, that player has merely called the $6 bet.

16. All wagers and calls of an improperly low amount must be brought up to proper size if the error is discovered before the betting round has been completed. This includes actions such as betting a lower amount than the minimum bring-in (other than going all-in) and betting the lower limit on an upper limit betting round. If a wager is supposed to be made in a rounded off amount, is not, and must be corrected, it shall be changed to the proper amount nearest in size. No one who has acted may change a call to a raise because the wager size has been changed.

3.6: THE SHOWDOWN

1. To win any part of a pot, a player must show all of his cards face-up on the table, whether they were used in the final hand played or not.

2. Cards speak (cards read for themselves). The dealer assists in reading hands, but players are responsible for holding onto their cards until the winner is declared. Although verbal declarations as to the contents of a hand are not binding, deliberately miscalling a hand with the intent of causing another player to discard a winning hand is unethical and may result in forfeiture of the pot. (For more information on miscalling a hand see 11.0: Lowball, Rule 15 and Rule 16.)

3. Any player, dealer or floorperson who sees an incorrect amount of chips put into the pot, or an error about to be made in awarding a pot, has an ethical obligation to point out the error. Please help keep mistakes of this nature to a minimum.

4. All losing hands will be killed by the dealer before a pot is awarded.

5. Any player who has been dealt in may request to see any hand that was eligible to participate in the showdown, even if the opponent's hand or the winning hand has been mucked. However, this is a privilege that may be revoked if abused. If a player other than the pot winner asks to see a hand that has been folded, that hand is

dead. If the winning player asks to see a losing player's hand, both hands are live, and the best hand wins.

6. Show one, show all. Players are entitled to receive equal access to information about the contents of another player's hand. After a deal, if cards are shown to another player, every player at the table has a right to see those cards. During a deal, cards that were shown to an active player who might have a further wagering decision on that betting round must immediately be shown to all the other players. If the player who saw the cards is not involved in the deal, or cannot use the information in wagering, the information should be withheld until the betting is over, so it does not affect the normal outcome of the deal. Cards shown to a person who has no more wagering decisions on that betting round, but might use the information on a later betting round, should be shown to the other players at the conclusion of that betting round. If only a portion of the hand has been shown, there is no requirement to show any of the unseen cards. The shown cards are treated as given in the preceding part of this rule.

7. If there is a side pot, the winner of that pot should be decided before the main pot is awarded. If there are multiple side pots, they are decided and awarded by having the pot with the players starting the deal with the greatest number of chips settled first, and so forth.

8. If everyone checks (or is all-in) on the final betting round, the player who acted first is the first to show the hand. If there is wagering on the final betting round, the last player to take aggressive action by a bet or raise is the first to show the hand. In order to speed up the game, a player holding a probable winner is encouraged to show the hand without delay. If there are one or more side pots (because someone is all-in), players are asked to aid in determining the pot winner by not showing their cards until a pot they are in is being settled.

3.7: TIES

1. The ranking of suits from highest to lowest is spades, hearts, diamonds, clubs. Suits never break a tie for winning a pot. Suits are used to break a tie between cards of the same rank (no redeal or redraw).

2. Dealing a card to each player is used to determine things like who moves to another table. If the cards are dealt, the order is clockwise starting with the first player on the dealer's left (the button position is irrelevant). Drawing a card is used to determine things like who

gets the button in a new game, or seating order coming from a broken game.

3. An odd chip will be broken down to the smallest unit used in the game.
4. No player may receive more than one odd chip.
5. If two or more hands tie, an odd chip will be awarded as follows:

   (a) In a button game, the first hand clockwise from the button gets the odd chip.

   (b) In a stud game, the odd chip will be given to the highest card by suit in all high games, and to the lowest card by suit in all low games. (When making this determination, all cards are used, not just the five cards that constitute the player's hand.)

   (c) In high-low split games, the high hand receives the odd chip in a split between the high and the low hands. The odd chip between tied high hands is awarded as in a high game of that poker form, and the odd chip between tied low hands is awarded as in a low game of that poker form. If two players have identical hands, the pot will be split as evenly as possible.

   (d) All side pots and the main pot will be split as separate pots, not mixed together.

4.0: BUTTON AND BLIND USE

In button games, a non-playing dealer normally does the actual dealing. A round disk called the button is used to indicate which player has the dealer position. The player with the button is last to receive cards on the initial deal and has the right of last action on all but the first betting round. The button moves one seat clockwise after a deal ends to rotate the advantage of last action. One or more blind bets are usually used to stimulate action and initiate play. Blinds are posted before the players look at their cards. Blinds are part of a player's bet (unless a certain structure or situation specifies otherwise). A blind other than the big blind may be treated as dead (not part of the poster's bet) in some structures, as when a special additional "dead blind" for the collection is specified by a cardroom. With two blinds, the small blind is posted by the first player clockwise from the button and the big blind is posted by the second player clockwise from the button. With more than two blinds, the smallest blind is normally left of the button (not on it). On the initial betting round, action starts with the first player to the left of the blinds. On all subsequent betting rounds, the action starts with the first active player to the left of the button.

RULES FOR USING BLINDS

1. The minimum bring-in and allowable raise sizes for the opener are specified by the poker form used and blind amounts set for a game. They remain the same even when the player in the blind does not have enough chips to post the full amount.

2. Each round every player must get an opportunity for the button, and meet the total amount of the blind obligations. Either of the following methods of button and blind placement may be designated to do this:

   (a) Moving button – The button always moves forward to the next player and the blinds adjust accordingly. There may be more than one big blind.

   (b) Dead button – The big blind is posted by the player due for it, and the small blind and button are positioned accordingly, even if this means the small blind or the button is placed in front of an empty seat, giving the same player the privilege of last action on consecutive hands. [See 16.0: Explanations, discussion #1, for more information on this rule.]

3. In heads-up play with two blinds, the small blind is on the button.

4. A new player entering the game has the following options:

   (a) Wait for the big blind.

   (b) Post an amount equal to the big blind and immediately be dealt a hand. (In lowball, a new player must either post an amount double the big blind or wait for the big blind.)

5. A new player who elects to let the button go by once without posting is not treated as a player in the game who has missed a blind, and needs to post only the big blind when entering the game.

6. A person playing over is considered to be a new player, and must post the amount of the big blind or wait for the big blind.

7. A new player cannot be dealt in between the big blind and the button. Blinds may not be made up between the big blind and the button. You must wait until the button passes. [See 16.0: Explanations, discussion #5, for more information on this rule.]

8. Chips posted by the big blind are treated as a bet.

9. A player posting a blind in the game's regular structure has the option of raising the pot at the first turn to act. This option to raise is retained if someone goes all-in with a wager of less than the minimum raise.

10. A player who misses any or all blinds can resume play by either posting all the blinds missed or waiting for the big blind. If you choose to post the total amount of the blinds, an amount up to the size of the minimum opening bet is live. The remainder is taken by the dealer to the center of the pot and is not part of your bet. When it is your next turn to act, you have the option to raise.

11. If a player who owes a blind (as a result of a missed blind) is dealt in without posting, the hand is dead if the player looks at it before putting up the required chips, and has not yet acted. If the player acts on the hand and plays it, putting chips into the pot before the error is discovered, the hand is live, and the player is required to post on the next deal.

12. A player who goes all-in and loses is obligated to make up the blinds if they are missed before a rebuy is made. (The person is not treated as a new player when reentering.)

13. These rules about blinds apply to a newly started game:
    (a) Any player who drew for the button is considered active in the game and is required to make up any missed blinds.
    (b) A new player will not be required to post a blind until the button has made one complete revolution around the table, provided a blind has not yet passed that seat.
    (c) A player may change seats without penalty, provided a blind has not yet passed the new seat.

14. If you move closer to the big blind, you can be dealt in without any penalty.

15. In all multiple-blind games, a player who changes seats will be dealt in on the first available hand in the same relative position. Example: If you move two active positions away from the big blind, you must wait two hands before being dealt in again. If you do not wish to wait and have not yet missed a blind, then you can post an amount equal to the big blind and receive a hand. (Exception: At lowball you must kill the pot, wait for the same relative position, or wait for the big blind; see 11.0: Lowball, rule #7.)

16. A player who "deals off" (by playing the button and then immediately getting up to change seats) can allow the blinds to pass the new seat one time and reenter the game behind the button without having to post a blind.

17. A live "straddle bet" is not allowed at limit poker except in specified games.

5.0: HOLD 'EM

In hold 'em, players receive two downcards as their personal hand (holecards), after which there is a round of betting. Three boardcards are turned simultaneously (called the "flop") and another round of betting occurs. The next two boardcards are turned one at a time, with a round of betting after each card. The boardcards are common cards used by all players, and a player may use any five-card combination from among the board and personal cards. A player may even use all of the boardcards and no personal cards to form a hand (play the board). A dealer button is used. The usual structure is to use two blinds, but it is possible to play the game with one blind, multiple blinds, an ante, or combination of blinds plus an ante.

RULES

These rules deal only with irregularities. See 4.0: Button and Blind Use, for rules on that subject.

1. If the initial holecard dealt to the first or second player is exposed, a misdeal results. The dealer will retrieve the card, reshuffle, and recut the cards. If any other holecard is exposed due to a dealer error, the deal continues. The exposed card may not be kept. After completing the hand, the dealer replaces the card with the top card on the deck, and the exposed card is then used for the burncard. If more than one holecard is exposed, this is a misdeal and there must be a redeal.

2. If the dealer mistakenly deals the first player an extra card (after all players have received their starting hands), the card will be returned to the deck and used for the burncard. If the dealer mistakenly deals more than one extra card, it is a misdeal.

3. If the flop contains too many cards, it must be redealt. (This applies even if it were possible to know which card was the extra one.)

4. If the dealer failed to burn a card before dealing the flop, or burned two cards, the error should be rectified by using the proper burncard and flop, if no boardcards were exposed. The deck must be reshuffled if any boardcards were exposed.

5. If the dealer burns and turns before a betting round is complete, the card(s) may not be used, even if all subsequent players elect to fold. Nobody has an option of accepting or rejecting the card. The betting is then completed, and the error rectified in the prescribed manner for that situation.

6. If the dealer fails to burn a card or burns more than one card, the error should be corrected if discovered before betting action has started for that round. Once action has been taken on a boardcard by any player, the card must stand. Whether the error is able to be corrected or not, subsequent cards dealt should be those that would have come if no error had occurred. For example, if two cards were burned, one of the cards should be put back on the deck and used for the burncard on the next round. If there was no betting on a round because a player was all-in, the error should be corrected if discovered before the pot has been awarded.

7. If the flop needs to be redealt for any reason, the boardcards are mixed with the remainder of the deck. The burncard remains on the table. After shuffling, the dealer cuts the deck and deals a new flop without burning a card. [See 16.0: Explanations, discussion #4, for more information on this rule.]

8. A dealing error for the fourth boardcard is rectified in a manner to least influence the identity of the boardcards that would have been used without the error. The dealer burns and deals what would have been the fifth card in the fourth card's place. After this round of betting, the dealer reshuffles the deck, including the card that was taken out of play, but not including the burncards or discards. The dealer then cuts the deck and deals the final card without burning a card. If the fifth card is turned up prematurely, the deck is reshuffled and dealt in the same manner. [See 16.0: Explanations, discussion #4, for more information on this rule.]

9. You must declare that you are playing the board before you throw your cards away. Otherwise, you relinquish all claim to the pot. (The rule for tournament play is you must retain your hand and show it if asked, in order to win part of the pot.)

6.0: OMAHA

Omaha is similar to hold 'em in using a three-card flop on the board, a fourth boardcard and then a fifth boardcard. Each player is dealt four holecards (instead of two) at the start. In order to make a valid hand, a player must use precisely two holecards with three boardcards. The betting is the same as in hold 'em, using a preflop, flop, turn and river betting rounds. At the showdown, the entire four-card hand should be shown to receive the pot.

RULES OF OMAHA

1. All the rules of hold 'em apply to Omaha except the rule on playing the board, which is not possible in Omaha (because you must use two cards from your hand and three cards from the board).

7.0: OMAHA HIGH-LOW

Omaha is often played high-low split. The player may use any combination of two holecards and three boardcards for the high hand and another (or the same) combination of two holecards and three boardcards for the low hand.

The rules governing kill pots are listed in 13.0: Kill Pots.

RULES OF OMAHA HIGH-LOW

1. All the rules of Omaha apply to Omaha high-low split except as below.
2. A qualifier of 8-or-better for low is used. This means to win the low half of the pot, a player's hand at the showdown must have five cards of different ranks that are an eight or lower in rank. (An ace is the highest card and also the lowest card.) If there is no qualifying hand for low, the best high hand wins the whole pot.
3. Straights and flushes do not impair the low value of a hand.

8.0: SEVEN-CARD STUD

Seven-card stud is played with a starting hand of two downcards and one upcard dealt before the first betting round. There are then three more upcards and a final downcard, with a betting round after each, for a total of five betting rounds on a deal played to the showdown. The best five-card poker hand wins the pot. In all fixed-limit games, the smaller bet is wagered for the first two betting rounds, and the larger bet is wagered for the last three betting rounds (on the fifth, sixth and seventh cards). If there is an open pair on the fourth card, any player has the option of making the smaller or larger bet. Deliberately changing the order of your upcards in a stud game is improper because it unfairly misleads the other players.

RULES OF SEVEN-CARD STUD

1. If your first or second holecard is accidentally turned up by the dealer, then your third card will be dealt down. If both holecards are dealt up, you have a dead hand and receive your ante back. If the first card dealt face-up would have been the lowcard, action starts with the first hand to that player's left. That player may fold, open for the forced bet, or open for a full bet. (In tournament play, if a downcard is dealt face-up, a misdeal is called.)
2. The first round of betting starts with a forced bet by the lowest upcard by suit. On subsequent betting rounds, the high hand on board initiates the action (a tie is broken by position, with the player who received cards first acting first).
3. The player with the forced bet has the option of opening for a full bet.
4. If the player with the lowcard is all-in for the ante, the person to that player's left acts first. If the player with the lowcard has only enough chips for a portion of the forced bet, the wager is made. All other players must enter for at least the normal amount in that structure.
5. When the wrong person is designated as low and bets, if the next player has not yet acted, the action will be corrected to the real lowcard, who now must bet. The incorrect lowcard takes back the wager. If the next hand has acted after the incorrect lowcard wager, the wager stands, action continues from there, and the real lowcard has no obligations.

6. Increasing the amount wagered by the opening forced bet up to a full bet does not count as a raise, but merely as a completion of the bet. For example: In $15-$30 stud, the lowcard opens for $5. If the next player increases the bet to $15 (completes the bet), up to three raises are then allowed when using a three-raise limit.

7. In all fixed-limit games, when an open pair is showing on fourth street (second upcard), any player has the option of betting either the lower or the upper limit. For example: In a $5-$10 game, if you have a pair showing and are the high hand, you may bet either $5 or $10. If you bet $5, any player then has the option to call $5, raise $5, or raise $10. If a $10 raise is made, then all other raises must be in increments of $10. If the player high with the open pair on fourth street checks, then subsequent players have the same options that were given to the player who was high.

8. If you are not present at the table when it is your turn to act, you forfeit your ante and your forced bet, if any. If you have not returned to the table in time to act, the hand will be killed when the betting reaches your seat. (In tournament play, the dealer is instructed to kill the hand of any absent player as soon as everyone has received their entire starting hand.)

9. If a hand is folded when there is no wager, that seat will continue to receive cards until the hand is killed as a result of a bet (so the fold does not affect who gets the cards to come).

10. When facing a wager, picking up your upcards without calling is a fold. This act has no significance at the showdown because betting is over; the hand is live until discarded.

11. A card dealt off the table is treated as an exposed card.

12. The dealer announces the lowcard, the high hand, all raises and all pairs. Dealers do not announce possible straights or flushes (except for specified low-stakes games).

13. If the dealer burns two cards for one round or fails to burn a card, the cards will be corrected, if at all possible, to their proper positions. If this should happen on a final downcard, and either a card intermingles with a player's other holecards or a player looks at the card, the player must accept that card.

14. If the dealer burns and deals one or more cards before a round of betting has been completed, the card(s) must be eliminated from play. After the betting for that round is completed, an additional card

for each remaining player still active in the hand is also eliminated from play (to later deal the same cards to the players who would have received them without the error). After that round of betting has concluded, the dealer burns a card and play resumes. The removed cards are held off to the side in the event the dealer runs out of cards. If the prematurely dealt card is the final downcard and has been looked at or intermingled with the player's other holecards, the player must keep the card, and on sixth street betting may not bet or raise (because the player now has all seven cards).

15. If there are not enough cards left in the deck for all players, all the cards are dealt except the last card, which is mixed with the burncards (and any cards removed from the deck, as in the previous rule). The dealer then scrambles and cuts these cards, burns again, and delivers the remaining downcards, using the last card if necessary. If there are not as many cards as players remaining without a card, the dealer does not burn, so that each player can receive a fresh card. If the dealer determines that there will not be enough fresh cards for all of the remaining players, then the dealer announces to the table that a common card will be used. The dealer will burn a card and turn one card face-up in the center of the table as a common card that plays in everyone's hand. The player who is now high using the common card initiates the action for the last round.

16. An all-in player should receive holecards dealt face-down, but if the final holecard to such a player is dealt face-up, the card must be kept, and the other players receive their normal card.

17. If the dealer turns the last card face-up to any player, the hand now high on the board using all the upcards will start the action. The following rules apply to the dealing of cards:

   (a) If there are more than two players, all remaining players receive their last card face-down. A player whose last card is face-up has the option of declaring all-in before betting action starts, meaning that the player does not put any more chips into the pot and subsequent betting by the other active players will be on the side.

   (b) If there are only two players remaining and the first player's final downcard is dealt face-up, the second player's final downcard will also be dealt face-up, and the betting proceeds as normal. In the event the first player's final card is dealt face-down and the opponent's final card is dealt face-up, the player with the face-up final card has the option of declaring all-in (before betting action starts).

18. A hand with more than seven cards is dead. A hand with less than seven cards at the showdown is dead, except any player missing a seventh card may have the hand ruled live. [See 16.0: Explanations, discussion #2, for more information on this rule.]

19. A player who calls a bet even though beaten by an opponent's upcards is not entitled to a refund. (The caller receives information about the opponent that is not available for free.)

9.0: SEVEN-CARD STUD LOW (RAZZ)

The lowest-ranking hand wins the pot. Aces are low only, and two aces are the lowest pair. The high card (aces are low) is required to make the forced bet on the first round; the low hand acts first on all subsequent rounds. Straights and flushes have no adverse effect on the low value of a hand, so the best possible hand is 5-4-3-2-A. An open pair does not affect the betting limit.

RULES OF RAZZ

1. All seven-card stud rules apply in razz except as otherwise noted.
2. The highest card by suit starts the action with a forced bet. The low hand acts first on all subsequent rounds. If the low hand is tied, the first player clockwise from the dealer starts the action.
3. Fixed-limit games use the lower limit on third and fourth streets and the upper limit on subsequent streets. An open pair does not affect the limit.
4. The dealer announces all pairs the first time they occur, except pairs of facecards, which are never announced.

10.0: SEVEN-CARD STUD HIGH-LOW

A qualifier of 8-or-better for low applies to all high-low split games. To win for low, a player's hand at the showdown must have five cards of different ranks that are an eight or lower. If there is no qualifier for low, the best high hand wins the whole pot. Any five cards may be used to make the best high hand, and the same or any other five cards to make the best low hand.

RULES OF SEVEN-CARD STUD HIGH-LOW

1. All rules for seven-card stud apply to seven-card stud high-low split, except as noted.
2. A player may use any five cards to make the best high hand and any five cards, whether the same as the high hand or not, to make the best low hand.
3. An ace is the highest card and also the lowest card.
4. The low card by suit initiates the action on the first round, with an ace counting as a high card for this purpose. On subsequent rounds, the high hand initiates the action. If the high hand is tied, the first player in the tie clockwise from the dealer acts first. If the high hand is all-in, action proceeds clockwise as if that person had checked.
5. Straights and flushes do not affect the value of a low hand.
6. Fixed-limit games use the lower limit on third and fourth streets and the upper limit on subsequent rounds. An open pair on fourth street does not affect the limit.
7. Splitting pots is determined only by the cards, and not by agreement among players.
8. When there is an odd chip in a pot, the chip goes to the high hand. If two players split the pot by tying for both the high and the low, the pot shall be split as evenly as possible, and the player with the highest card by suit receives the odd chip. When making this determination, all cards are used, not just the five cards used for the final hand played.
9. When there is one odd chip in the high portion of the pot and two or more high hands split all or half the pot, the odd chip goes to the player with the high card by suit. When two or more low hands split half the pot, the odd chip goes to the player with the low card by suit.

11.0: LOWBALL

Lowball is draw poker with the lowest hand winning the pot. Each player is dealt five cards face-down, after which there is a betting round. Players are required to open with a bet or fold. The players who remain in the pot after the first betting round now have an option to improve their hand by replacing cards in their hands with new ones. This is the draw. The game is normally played with one or more blinds, sometimes with an ante added. Some betting structures allow the big blind to be called; other structures require the minimum open to be double the big blind. In limit poker, the usual structure has the limit double after the draw (Northern California is an exception). The most popular forms of lowball are ace-to-five lowball (also known as California lowball), and deuce-to-seven lowball (also known as Kansas City lowball). Ace-to-five lowball gets its name because the best hand at that form is 5-4-3-2-A. Deuce-to-seven lowball gets its name because the best hand at that form is 7-5-4-3-2 (not of the same suit). For a further description of the forms of lowball, please see the individual section for each game. All rules governing kill pots are listed in 13.0: Kill Pots.

RULES OF LOWBALL

1. The rules governing misdeals for hold 'em and other button games will be used for lowball. [See 16.0: Explanations, discussion #7, for more information on this rule.] These rules governing misdeals are reprinted here for convenience.

"The following circumstances cause a misdeal, provided attention is called to the error before two players have acted on their hands:

    (a) The first or second card of the hand has been exposed by a dealer error.

    (b) Two or more cards have been exposed by the dealer.

    (c) Two or more extra cards have been dealt in the starting hands of a game.

    (d) An incorrect number of cards has been dealt to a player, except the button may receive one more card to complete a starting hand.

    (e) The button was out of position.

    (f) The first card was dealt to the wrong position.

    (g) Cards have been dealt out of the proper sequence.

    (h) Cards have been dealt to an empty seat or a player not entitled to a hand.

    (i) A player has been dealt out who is entitled to a hand. This player must be present at the table or have posted a blind or ante."

2. In limit play, a bet and four raises are allowed in multihanded pots. [See 16.0: Explanations, discussion #6, for more information on this rule.]

3. As a new player, you have two options:

    (a) To wait for the big blind.

    (b) To kill the pot for double the amount of the big blind.

4. In a single-blind game, a player who has less than half a blind may receive a hand. However, the next player is obligated to take the blind. If the all-in player wins the pot or buys in again, that player will then be obligated to either take the blind on the next deal or sit out until due for the big blind.

5. In single-blind games, half a blind or more constitutes a full blind.

6. In single-blind games, if you fail to take the blind, you may only be dealt in on the blind.

7. In multiple-blind games, if the big blind passes your seat, you may either wait for the big blind or kill the pot in order to receive a hand. This does not apply if you have taken all of your blinds and changed seats. In this situation, you may be dealt in as soon as your position relative to the blinds entitles you to a hand (the button may go by you once without penalty).

8. Before the draw, whether an exposed card must be taken depends on the form of lowball being played; see that form. (The player never has an option.)

9. On the draw, an exposed card cannot be taken. The draw is completed to each player in order, and then the exposed card is replaced.

10. A player may draw up to four consecutive cards. If a player wishes to draw five new cards, four are dealt right away, and the fifth card after everyone else has drawn cards. If the last player wishes to draw five new cards, four are dealt right away, and a card is burned before the player receives a fifth card. [See 16.0: Explanations, discussion #9, for more information about this rule.]

11. You may change the number of cards you wish to draw, provided:
    (a) No card has been dealt off the deck in response to your request (including the burncard).
    (b) No player has acted, in either the betting or indicating the number of cards to be drawn, based on the number of cards you have requested.

12. Five cards constitute a playing hand; more or fewer than five cards after the draw constitutes a fouled hand. Before the draw, if you have fewer than five cards in your hand, you may receive additional cards, provided no action has been taken by the first player to act (unless that action occurs before the deal is completed). However, the dealer position may still receive a missing fifth card, even if action has taken place. If action has been taken, you are entitled on the draw to receive the number of cards necessary to complete a five-card hand.

13. If you are asked how many cards you drew by another active player, you are obligated to respond until there has been action after the draw, and the dealer is also obligated to respond. Once there is any action after the draw, you are no longer obliged to respond and the dealer cannot respond.

14. Rapping the table in turn constitutes either a pass or the declaration of a pat hand that does not want to draw any cards, depending on the situation.

15. Cards speak (cards read for themselves). However, you are not allowed to claim a better hand than you hold. (Example: If a player calls an "8", that player must produce at least an "8" low or better to win. But if a player erroneously calls the second card incorrectly, such as "8-6" when actually holding an 8-7, no penalty applies.) If you miscall your hand and cause another player to foul his or her hand, your hand is dead. If both hands remain intact, the best hand wins. If a miscalled hand occurs in a multihanded pot, the miscalled hand is dead, and the best remaining hand wins the pot. For your own protection, always hold your hand until you see your opponent's cards.

16. Any player spreading a hand with a pair in it must announce "pair" or risk losing the pot if it causes any other player to foul a hand. If two or more hands remain intact, the best hand wins the pot.

11.1: ACE-TO-FIVE LOWBALL

In ace-to-five lowball, the best hand is any 5-4-3-2-A. An ace is the lowest-ranking card. For hands with a pair, A-A beats 2-2. Straights and flushes do not count against your hand.

1. If a joker is used, it becomes the lowest card not present in your hand. The joker is assumed to be in use unless the contrary is posted.
2. In limit play, check-raise is not permitted (unless the players are alerted that it is allowed).
3. In limit ace-to-five lowball, before the draw, an exposed card of seven or under must be taken, and an exposed card higher than a seven must be replaced after the deal has been completed. This first exposed card is used as the burncard. [See 16.0: Explanations, discussion #8, for more information on this rule.]
4. In limit play, the "sevens rule" is assumed to be in use (the players should be alerted if it is not). If you check a seven or better and it is the best hand, all action after the draw is void, and you cannot win any money on any subsequent bets. You are still eligible to win whatever existed in the pot before the draw if you have the best hand. If you check a seven or better and the hand is beaten, you lose the pot and any additional calls you make. If there is an all-in bet after the draw that is less than half a bet, a seven or better may just call and win that bet. However, if another player overcalls this short bet and loses, the person who overcalls receives the bet back. If the seven or better completes to a full bet, this fulfills all obligations.

11.2: DEUCE-TO-SEVEN LOWBALL

In deuce-to-seven lowball (sometimes known as Kansas City lowball), in most respects, the worst conventional poker hand wins. Straights and flushes count against you, crippling the value of a hand. The ace is used only as a high card. Therefore, the best hand is 7-5-4-3-2, not all of the same suit. The hand 5-4-3-2-A is not considered to be a straight, but an ace-5 high, so it beats other ace-high hands and pairs, but loses to king-high. A pair of aces is the highest pair, so it loses to any other pair.

The rules for deuce-to-seven lowball are the same as those for ace-to-five lowball, except for the following differences:

1. The best hand is 7-5-4-3-2 of at least two different suits. Straights and flushes count against you, and aces are considered high only.

2. Before the draw, an exposed card of 7, 5, 4, 3, or 2 must be taken. Any other exposed card must be replaced (including a 6).
3. Check-raise is allowed on any hand after the draw.
4. After the draw, a seven or better is not required to bet.

11.3: NO-LIMIT AND POT-LIMIT LOWBALL

1. All the rules for no-limit and pot-limit poker (see 14.0: No-Limit and Pot-Limit) apply to no-limit and pot-limit lowball. All other lowball rules apply, except as noted.

   A player is not entitled to know that an opponent does not hold the best possible hand, so these rules for exposed cards before the draw apply:
   - (a) In ace-to-five lowball, a player must take an exposed card of A, 2, 3, 4, or 5, and any other card must be replaced.
   - (b) In deuce-to-seven lowball, the player must take an exposed card of 2, 3, 4, 5, or 7, and any other card including a 6 must be replaced.

   After the draw, any exposed card must be replaced.
4. After the draw, a player may check any hand without penalty (The sevens rule is not used).
5. Check-raise is allowed.

12.0: DRAW HIGH

There are two betting rounds, one before the draw and one after the draw. The game is played with a button and an ante. Players in turn may check, open for the minimum, or open with a raise. After the first betting round the players have the opportunity to draw new cards to replace the ones they discard. Action after the draw starts with the opener, or next player proceeding clockwise if the opener has folded. The betting limit after the draw is twice the amount of the betting limit before the draw. Some draw high games allow a player to open on anything; others require the opener to have a pair of jacks or better.

RULES OF DRAW HIGH

1. A maximum of a bet and four raises is permitted in multihanded pots. [See 16.0: Explanations, discussion #6, for more information on this rule.]
2. Check-raise is permitted both before and after the draw.
3. The rules governing misdeals for hold 'em and other button games will be used for draw.
4. Any card that is exposed by the dealer before the draw must be kept.
5. Five cards constitute a playing hand. Less than five cards for a player (other than the button) before action has been taken is a misdeal. If action has been taken, a player with fewer than five cards may draw the number of cards necessary to complete a five-card hand. The button may receive the fifth card even if action has taken place. More or fewer than five cards after the draw constitutes a fouled hand.
6. A player may draw up to four consecutive cards. If a player wishes to draw five new cards, four are dealt right away, and the fifth card after everyone else has drawn cards. If the last player wishes to draw five new cards, four are dealt right away, and a card is burned before the player receives a fifth card. [See 16.0: Explanations, discussion #9, for more information about this rule.]
7. You may change the number of cards you wish to draw, provided:
   (a) No cards have been dealt off the deck in response to your request (including the burncard).
   (b) No player has acted, in either the betting or indicating the number of cards to be drawn, based on the number of cards you have requested.
8. On the draw, an exposed card cannot be taken. The draw is completed to each player in order, and then the exposed card is replaced.
9. If you are asked how many cards you drew by another active player, you are obligated to respond until there has been action after the draw, and the dealer is also obligated to respond. Once there is any action after the draw, you are no longer obliged to respond and the dealer cannot respond.
10. Rapping the table in turn constitutes either a pass or the declaration of a pat hand that does not want to draw any cards, depending on the situation. A player who indicates a pat hand by rapping the

table, not knowing the pot has been raised, may still play his or her hand.

11. You may not change your seat between hands when there are multiple antes or forfeited money in the pot.

12. You have the right to pay the ante (whether single or multiple) at any time and receive a hand, unless there is any additional money in the pot that has been forfeited during a hand in which you were not involved.

13. If the pot has been declared open by an all-in player playing for just the antes, all callers must come in for the full opening bet.

14. If you have only a full ante and no other chips on the table, you may play for just the antes. If no one opens and there is another ante, you may still play for that part of the antes that you have matched, without putting in any more money.

12.1: THE JOKER

1. The players will be alerted as to whether the joker is in use.

2. The joker may be used only as an ace, or to complete a straight, flush, or straight flush. (Thus it is not a completely wild card.)

3. If the joker is used to make a flush, it will be the highest card of the flush not present in the hand.

4. Five aces is the best possible hand (four aces and joker).

13.0: KILL POTS

To kill a pot means to post an overblind that increases the betting limit. A full kill is double the amount of the big blind, and doubles the betting limits. A half kill is one-and-a-half times the big blind, and increases the betting limits by that amount. A kill may be optional in a game, and is often used at lowball when a player wants to be dealt in right away instead of waiting to take the big blind. A kill may be required in a game for any time a specified event takes place. In high-low split games using a required kill, a player who scoops a pot bigger than a set size must kill the next pot. In other games using a required kill, a player who wins two consecutive pots must kill the next pot. In this type of kill game, a marker called a "kill button" indicates which player has won the pot, and the winner keeps this marker until the next hand is completed. If the player who has the kill button wins a second consecutive pot and it qualifies monetarily, that player must kill the next pot.

RULES OF KILL POTS

1. The kill button is neutral (belonging to no player) if:
    (a) It is the first hand of a new game.
    (b) The winner of the previous pot has quit the game.
    (c) The previous pot was split and neither player had the kill button.
2. In a kill pot, the killer acts in proper turn (after the person on the immediate right).
3. There is no pot-size requirement for the first pot or "leg" of a kill. For the second "leg" to qualify for a kill, you must win at least one full bet for whatever limit you are playing, and it cannot be any part of the blind structure.
4. If a player with one "leg up" splits the next pot, that player still has a "leg up" for the next hand. If the player who split the pot was the kill in the previous hand, then that player must also kill the next pot.
5. A person who leaves the table with a "leg up" toward a kill still has a "leg up" upon returning to the game.
6. A player who is required to post a kill must do so that same hand even if wishing to quit or be dealt out. A player who fails to post a required kill blind will not be allowed to participate in any game until the kill money is posted.
7. Kill blinds are considered part of the pot. If a player with a required kill wins again, then that player must kill it again (for the same amount as the previous hand).
8. When a player wins both the high and the low pot ("scoops") in a split-pot game with a kill provision, the next hand will be killed only if the pot is at least five times the size of the upper limit of the game.
9. If you are unaware that the pot has been killed and put in a lesser amount, if it is a required kill pot with the kill button face-up, you must put in the correct amount. If not, you may withdraw the chips and reconsider your action.
10. In lowball, an optional rule is allowing players to look at their first two cards and then opt whether to kill the pot. The pot may no longer be killed if any player in the game has received a third card.

In order to kill the pot voluntarily, you must have at least four times the amount of the kill blind in your stack. For example: If the big blind is two chips, and the kill blind is four chips, the voluntary killer must have at least 16 chips prior to posting the kill. If this rule is used, it is in conjunction with having the killer act last on the first betting round rather than in proper order.

11. Only one kill is allowed per deal.

12. A new player is not entitled to play in a killed pot, but may do so by agreeing to kill the next pot.

13. Broken game status is allowed only for players of the same limit and game type. For this purpose, a game with a required kill is considered a different type of game than an otherwise similar game without a required kill.

14.0: NO LIMIT AND POT-LIMIT

A no-limit or pot-limit betting structure for a game gives it a different character from limit poker, requiring a separate set of rules in many situations. All the rules for limit games apply to no-limit and pot-limit games, except as noted in this section. No-limit means that the amount of a wager is limited only by the table stakes rule, so any part or all of a player's chips may be wagered. The rules of no-limit play also apply to pot-limit play, except that a bet may not exceed the pot size. The player is responsible for determining the pot size at no-limit, not the dealer. The dealer is responsible for determining the pot size at pot-limit, and should enforce the pot-size cap on wagers without waiting to be asked to do so by a player. For those rules that apply only to no-limit and pot-limit lowball, see the sub-section at the end of 11.0: Lowball.

14.1: NO-LIMIT RULES

1. The number of raises in any betting round is unlimited.

2. The minimum bet size is the amount of the minimum bring-in, unless the player is going all-in. The minimum bring-in is the size of the big blind unless the structure of the game is preset by the house to some other amount (such as double the big blind). The minimum bet remains the same amount on all betting rounds. If the big blind

does not have sufficient chips to post the required amount, a player who enters the pot on the initial betting round is still required to enter for at least the minimum bet (unless going all-in for a lesser sum) and a preflop raiser must at least double the size of the big blind. At all other times, when someone goes all-in for less than the minimum bet, a player has the option of just calling the all-in amount. If a player goes all-in for an amount that is less than the minimum bet, a player who wishes to raise must raise at least the amount of the minimum bet. For example, if the minimum bet is $100, and a player goes all-in on the flop for $20, a player may fold, call $20, or raise to at least a total of $120.

3. All raises must be equal to or greater than the size of the previous bet or raise on that betting round, except for an all-in wager. Example: Player A bets 100 and player B raises to 200. Player C wishing to raise must raise at least 100 more, making the total bet at least 300. A player who has already acted and is not facing a fullsize wager may not subsequently raise an all-in bet that is less than the minimum bet or less than the full size of the last bet or raise. (The half-the-size rule for reopening the betting is for limit poker only.)

4. Multiple all-in wagers, each of an amount too small to qualify as a raise, still act as a raise and reopen the betting if the resulting wager size to a player qualifies as a raise. Example: Player A bets $100 and Player B raises $100 more, making the total bet $200. If Player C goes all in for less than $300 total (not a full $100 raise), and Player A calls, then Player B has no option to raise again, because he wasn't fully raised. (Player A could have raised, because Player B raised.)

5. "Completing the bet" is a limit poker wager type only, and not used at big-bet poker.

6. At non-tournament play, a player who says "raise" is allowed to continue putting chips into the pot with more than one move; the wager is assumed complete when the player's hands come to rest outside the pot area. (This rule is used because no-limit play may require a large number of chips be put into the pot.) In tournament play, the TDA rules require that the player either use a verbal statement giving the amount of the raise or put the chips into the pot in a single motion, to avoid making a string-bet.

7. A wager is not binding until the chips are actually released into the pot, unless the player has made a verbal statement of action.

8. If there is a discrepancy between a player's verbal statement and the amount put into the pot, the bet will be corrected to the verbal statement.

9. If a call is short due to a counting error, the amount must be corrected, even if the bettor has shown down a superior hand.

10. A bet of a single chip or bill without comment is considered to be the full amount of the chip or bill allowed. However, a player acting on a previous bet with a larger denomination chip or bill is calling the previous bet unless this player makes a verbal declaration to raise the pot. (This includes acting on the forced bet of the big blind.)

11. If a player tries to bet or raise less than the legal minimum and has more chips, the wager must be increased to the proper size (but no greater). This does not apply to a player who has unintentionally put too much in to call.

12. Because the amount of a wager at big-bet poker has such a wide range, a player who has taken action based on a gross misunderstanding of the amount wagered may receive some protection by the decision-maker. A "call" or "raise" may be ruled not binding if it is obvious that the player grossly misunderstood the amount wagered, provided no damage has been caused by that action. Example: Player A bets $300, player B reraises to $1200, and Player C puts $300 into the pot and says, "call." It is obvious that player C believes the bet to be only $300 and he should be allowed to withdraw his $300 and reconsider his wager. A bettor should not show down a hand until the amount put into the pot for a call seems reasonably correct, or it is obvious that the caller understands the amount wagered. The decision-maker is allowed considerable discretion in ruling on this type of situation. A possible rule-of-thumb is to disallow any claim of not understanding the amount wagered if the caller has put eighty percent or more of that amount into the pot.

> Example: On the end, a player puts a $500 chip into the pot and says softly, "Four hundred." The opponent puts a $100 chip into the pot and says, "Call." The bettor immediately shows the

hand. The dealer says, "He bet four hundred." The caller says, "Oh, I thought he bet a hundred." In this case, the recommended ruling normally is that the bettor had an obligation to not show the hand when the amount put into the pot was obviously short, and the "call" can be retracted. Note that the character of each player can be a factor. (Unfortunately, situations can arise at big-bet poker that are not so clear-cut as this.)

13. All wagers may be required to be in the same denomination of chip (or larger) used for the minimum bring-in, even if smaller chips are used in the blind structure. If this is done, the smaller chips do not play except in quantity, even when going all-in.

14. Since all a player's chips may be put at risk on a hand, the house has the right to set a maximum amount for the buy-in to help control the effective size of a game.

15. In non-tournament games, one optional live straddle is allowed. The player who posts the straddle has last action for the first round of betting and is allowed to raise. To straddle, a player must be on the immediate left of the big blind, and must post an amount twice the size of the big blind. A straddle bet sets a new minimum bring-in; it is not treated as a raise.

16. In all no-limit and pot-limit games, the house has the right to place a maximum time limit for taking action on your hand. The clock may be put on someone by the dealer as directed by a floorperson, if a player requests it. If the clock is put on you when you are facing a bet, you will have one additional minute to act on your hand. You will have a ten-second warning, after which your hand is dead if you have not acted.

17. The cardroom does not condone "insurance" or any other "proposition" wagers. The management declines to make decisions in such matters, and the pot will be awarded to the best hand. Players are asked to refrain from instigating proposition wagers in any form. The players are allowed to agree to deal twice (or three times) when someone is all-in. "Dealing twice" means the pot is divided in two, with each portion being dealt for separately.

14.2: POT-LIMIT RULES

A bet may not exceed the pot size. The maximum amount a player can raise is the amount in the pot after the call is made. Therefore, if a pot is $100, and someone makes a $50 bet, the next player can call $50 and raise the pot $200, for a total wager of $250.

1. If a wager is made that exceeds the pot size, the surplus will be given back to the bettor as soon as possible, and the amount will be reduced to the maximum allowable.

2. The dealer or any player in the game can and should call attention to a wager that appears to exceed the pot size (this also applies to heads-up pots). The oversize wager may be corrected at any point until all players have acted on it.

3. If an oversize wager has stood for a length of time with someone considering what action to take, that person has had to act on a wager that was thought to be a certain size. If the player then decides to call or raise, and attention is called at this late point to whether this is an allowable amount, the floorperson may rule that the oversize amount must stand (especially if the person now trying to reduce the amount is the person that made the wager).

4. In pot-limit play, it is advisable in many structures to round off the pot size upward to produce a faster pace of play. This is done by treating any odd amount as the next larger size. For example, if the pot size was being kept track of with $25 units, then a pot size of $80 would be treated as a pot size of $100.

5. In pot-limit hold 'em and pot-limit Omaha money games, many structures treat the little blind as if it were the same size of the big blind in computing pot size. In such a structure, a player can open for a maximum of four times the size of the big blind. For example, if the blinds are $5 and $10, a player may open with a raise to $40. (The range of options is to either open with a call of $10, or raise in increments of five dollars to any amount from $20 to $40.) Subsequent players also treat the $5 as if it were $10 in computing the pot size, until the big blind is through acting on the first betting round. This rule of treating the little blind as if it were the size of the big blind is especially desirable in a structure where the little blind uses a lower-denomination chip than the big blind, as in using blinds of $10 and $25 (two $5 chips and a $25 chip). At tournament play, strict pot-limit rules are normally used,

so there the maximum opening wager is 3.5 times the size of the big blind.

6. In pot-limit, a player who puts a chip or a bill larger than the pot size into the pot without comment is considered to be making a bet of the pot size (unless he is facing a bet).

15.0: TOURNAMENTS

By participating in a tournament, you agree to abide by the rules and behave in a courteous manner. A violator may be verbally warned, suspended from play for a specified length of time, or disqualified from the tournament. Chips from a disqualified participant will be removed from play. Players, whether in the hand or not, may not discuss the hands until the action is complete. Players are obligated to protect the other players in the tournament at all times. Discussing cards discarded or hand possibilities is not allowed. A penalty may be given for discussion of hands during the play.

1. Whenever possible, all rules are the same as those that apply to live games.
2. Initial seating is determined by random draw or assignment. (For a one-table satellite event, cards to determine seating may be left face-up so the earlier entrants can pick their seat, since the button is assigned randomly.)
3. A change of seat is not allowed after play starts, except as assigned by the director.
4. The appropriate starting amount of chips will be placed on the table for each paid entrant at the beginning of the event, whether the person is present or not.
5. If a paid entrant is absent at the start of an event, at some point an effort will be made to locate and contact the player. If the player requests the chips be left in place until arrival, the request will be honored. If the player is unable to be contacted, the chips may be removed from play at the discretion of the director anytime after a new betting level is begun or a half-hour has elapsed, whichever occurs first.

6. A starting stack of chips may be placed in a seat to accommodate late entrants (so all antes and blinds have been appropriately paid). An unsold seat will have such a stack removed at a time left to the discretion of the director.

7. A no-show or absent player is always dealt a hand. That player's stack will post chips for blinds and antes, and have the forced lowcard bet put into the pot at stud.

8. In all tournament games using a dealer button, the starting position of the button is determined by the players drawing for the high card.

9. Limits and blinds are raised at regularly scheduled intervals.

10. If there is a signal designating the end of a betting level, the new limits apply on the next deal. (A deal begins with the first riffle of the shuffle.)

11. The lowest denomination of chip in play will be removed from the table when it is no longer needed in the blind or ante structure. All lower-denomination chips that are of sufficient quantity for a new chip will be changed up directly. The method for removal of odd chips is to deal one card to a player for each odd chip possessed. Cards are dealt clockwise starting with the 1-seat, with each player receiving all cards before any cards are dealt to the next player. A player may not be eliminated from the event by the chip-change process. If a player has no chips after the race has been held, he will be given a chip of the higher denomination before anyone else is awarded a chip. Next, the player with the highest card by suit gets enough odd chips to exchange for one new chip, the second-highest card gets to exchange for the next chip, and so forth, until all the lower-denomination chips are exchanged. If an odd number of lower-denomination chips are left after this process, the player with the highest card remaining will receive a new chip if he has half or more of the quantity of lower-denomination chips needed, otherwise nothing.

12. A player must be present at the table to stop the action by calling "time."

13. A player must be at the table by the time all players have their complete starting hands in order to have a live hand for that deal. (The dealer has been instructed to kill the hands of all absent players immediately after dealing each player a starting hand.)

14. As players are eliminated, tables are broken in a pre-set order, with players from the broken tables assigned to empty seats at other tables.

15. In button games, if a player is needed to move from a table to balance tables, the player due for the big blind will be automatically selected to move, and will be given the earliest seat due for the big blind if more than one seat is open.

16. New players to a table as a result of balancing tables are dealt in immediately unless they are in the small blind or button position, where they must wait until the button has passed to the player on their left.

17. The number of players at each table will be kept reasonably balanced by the transfer of a player as needed. With more than six tables, table size will be kept within two players. With six tables or less, table size will be kept within one player.

18. In all events, there is a redraw for seating when the field is reduced to three tables, two tables, and one table. (Redrawing at three tables is not mandatory in small tournaments with only four or five starting tables.)

19. If a player lacks sufficient chips for a blind or a forced bet, the player is entitled to get action on whatever amount of money is left in his stack. A player who posts a short blind and wins does not need to make up the blind.

20. A player who declares all in and loses the pot, then discovers that one or more chips were hidden, is not entitled to benefit from this. That player is eliminated from the tournament if the opponent had sufficient chips to cover the hidden ones (A rebuy is okay if allowable by the rules of that event). If another deal has not yet started, the director may rule the chips belong to the opponent who won that pot, if that obviously would have happened with the chips out in plain view. If the next deal has started, the discovered chips are removed from the tournament.

21. All players must leave their seat immediately after being eliminated from an event.

22. Showing cards from a live hand during the action injures the rights of other players still competing in an event, who wish to see contestants eliminated. A player in a multihanded pot may not show any cards during a deal. Heads-up, a player may not show

any cards unless the event has only two remaining players, or is winner-take-all. If a player deliberately shows a card, the player may be penalized (but his hand will not be ruled dead). Verbally stating one's hand during the play may be penalized.

23. The limitation on the number of raises at limit poker is also applied to heads-up situations (except the last two players in a tournament are exempted from a limitation on raises).

24. At pot-limit and no-limit play, the player must either use a verbal statement giving the amount of the raise or put chips into the pot in a single motion. Otherwise, it is a string bet.

25. Non-tournament chips are not allowed on the table.

26. Higher-denomination chips must be placed where they are easily visible to all other players.

27. All tournament chips must remain visible on the table throughout the event. Chips taken off the table will be removed from the event, and a player doing this may be disqualified.

28. Inappropriate behavior like throwing cards that go off the table may be punished with a penalty such as being dealt out for a length of time or number of hands. A severe infraction such as abusive or disruptive behavior may be punished by eviction from the tournament.

29. The decks is changed only when dealers change, unless a card is damaged.

30. The dealer button remains in position until the appropriate blinds are taken. Players must post all blinds every round. Because of this, last action may be given to the same player for two consecutive hands by the use of a "dead button." [See 16.0: Explanations, discussion #1, for more information on this rule.]

31. In heads-up play with two blinds, the small blind is on the button.

32. At stud, if a downcard on the initial hand is dealt face-up, a misdeal is called.

33. If a player announces the intent to rebuy before cards are dealt, that player is playing behind and is obligated to make the rebuy.

34. All hands will be turned face-up whenever a player is all-in and betting action is complete.

35. If multiple players go broke on the same hand, the player starting the hand with the larger amount of chips finishes in the higher place for prize money and any other award. Players eliminated on

the same deal who start their final hand with an equal amount of chips receive equal prize money, with the best hand on that deal receiving any non-divisible award.

36. Management is not required to rule on any private deals, side bets, or redistribution of the prize pool among finalists.

37. Private agreements by remaining players in an event regarding distribution of the prize pool are not condoned. (However, if such an agreement is made, the director has the option of ensuring that it is carried out by paying those amounts.) Any private agreement that does not include one or more active competitors is improper by definition.

38. A tournament event is expected to be played until completion. A private agreement that removes all prize money from being at stake in the competition is unethical.

39. Management retains the right to cancel any event, or alter it in a manner fair to the players.

16.0: EXPLANATIONS

1. The only place in this set of rules that an alternative is mentioned other than in this section is in the method of button and blind placement. That rule (the first rule in 4.0: Button and Blind Use) is repeated in an abbreviated version below for convenience.

"Each round all players must get the button, and meet the total amount of the blind obligations. Either of the following methods of button and blind placement may be used:

(a) Moving button – The button always moves forward to the next player and the blinds adjust accordingly. There may be more than one big blind.

(b) Dead button – The big blind is posted by the player due for it, and the small blind and button are positioned accordingly, even if this means the small blind or the button is placed in front of an empty seat, giving a player last action on consecutive hands."

Poker tradition has a lot to do with the fact that both of these methods are in widespread use, but neither method is superior in all situations. The moving button makes sure no player gets the advantage of last action twice on a round (a big advantage at no-limit or pot-limit play). On the other hand, a player may get to post a blind when on the button, which is more advantageous than posting in front of the button. The moving button creates a situation where two big blinds may be posted on a deal, which speeds up the action. At tournament play this speed-up can be undesirable, as when dealing is being done hand-for-hand to balance the pace of play between two remaining tables. A cardroom may either decide for the sake of simplicity to use only one method, or decide to tailor the method to the game and situation.

2. Most poker rule sets say you have a dead hand at the showdown if you do not have the proper number of cards for that game. At stud, this rule is too strict. An inexperienced player sometimes does not pay sufficient attention to the final card when holding a big hand like a flush or full house (where improvement is neither likely to happen nor be needed), and fails to protect that card. If the dealer erroneously puts that final card into the muck after the player fails to take it in, the rules should give the decision-maker an option to rule such a hand live. 8.0: Seven-Card Stud, rule #18, reads as below:

"A hand with more than seven cards is dead. A hand with less than seven cards at the showdown is dead, except any player missing a seventh card may have the hand ruled live."

3. This rulebook requires all cash to be changed into chips. In some cardrooms this may be impractical. If the cardroom chooses to allow cash, only $100 bills should be permitted.

4. The rules given for rectifying a hold 'em situation where the dealer has dealt the flop or another boardcard before all the betting action on a round are inferior, because the dealer is told to not burn a card on a redeal. Since the "no burn" rule is so common, there was no choice but to use it here. It would be better for poker if the rule were changed to always burning a card. Here are these rules (the third rule and fourth rule in 5.0: Hold 'Em).

"If the cards are flopped before the betting is complete, or if the flop contains too many cards, the boardcards are mixed with the remainder of the deck. The burncard remains on the table. After shuffling, the dealer cuts the deck and deals a new flop without burning a card."

"If the dealer turns the fourth card on the board before the betting round is complete, the card is taken out of play for that round, even if subsequent players elect to fold. The betting is then completed. The dealer burns and turns what would have been the fifth card in the fourth card's place. After this round of betting, the dealer reshuffles the deck, including the card that was taken out of play, but not including the burncards or discards. The dealer then cuts the deck and turns up the final card without burning a card.

The portion of this rule saying the dealer does not burn a card on the redeal is inferior. It is harder for the dealer to control the card to be dealt if a burn is required. The sentence in the rule should read, "The dealer then cuts the deck, burns a card, and turns the final card."

The present method for handling a premature dealing on the turn is used to have what would have been the last board-card used on the turn, and not reshuffling the deck until just before the last card is dealt. This method has four-fifths of the boardcards remaining the same, albeit in a different order. It would be better to reshuffle before the turn, preserving the chance of receiving the prematurely dealt card on either of the last two cards, as opposed to cutting that chance in half. The superiority of reshuffling right away is illustrated if the prematurely dealt card makes a gutshot straight-flush for a player.

5. Rule 7 in 4.0: Button and Blind Use says, "A new player cannot be dealt in between the big blind and the button. Blinds may not be made up between the big blind and the button. You must wait until the button passes." This rule is standard practice, but allowing a new player or player making up blinds to come in between the blinds is better (if dealers are trained how to handle the resulting situations), because it gets players eager to join or rejoin the game into action faster.

6. Most poker rulebooks follow the usual California practice in multihanded pots at limit poker of allowing a bet and six raises for lowball and draw high. The number of allowable raises for those games is given in this rulebook as a bet and four raises because this cuts down on the effect of collusion between players, and more raises than four are hardly ever needed to define the strength of two hands when another player is calling.

7. Lowball has historically had less stringent demands on the order of cards or acceptability of exposed cards than in most other poker forms. This rulebook follows the modern trend at lowball regarding misdeals of requiring the cards to be dealt face-down and in proper order.

8. At ace-to-five limit lowball, an exposed card rule used less often, but probably a superior rule, is to not let a player take an exposed six or seven (the rule for no-limit ace-to-five lowball). If a player gets to keep only a card that might make a perfect hand, having a card exposed is less advantageous, and the opponent must consider the chance of a perfect hand.

9. At lowball and draw high, some rule sets allow a player to draw five consecutive cards. The rule used here disallowing this makes cheating more difficult. Our rule #10 in lowball and rule #5 in draw high says, "A player may draw up to four consecutive cards. If a player wishes to draw five new cards, four are dealt right away, and the fifth card after everyone else has drawn cards. If the last player wishes to draw five new cards, four are dealt right away, and a card is burned before the player receives a fifth card."

ROBERT'S RULES OF POKER FOR PRIVATE GAMES

This version of Robert's Rules of Poker is for private games.
Reprinted courtesy of Bob Ciaffone.

Anyone contemplating the hosting of a private game should make sure what he is doing is not in violation of the law. Most laws governing private poker games are made at the state level. No state in our country allows a person to run a poker game as a business. Raking pots and charging an hourly rate for playing are two examples of activities only a licensed commercial cardroom would be allowed to do. Some states prohibit the playing of poker for money, because they prohibit any kind of gambling. Other states allow social gambling. Even though gambling laws may sometimes be enforced only sporadically, they do exist, and people are prosecuted for violating them. Check out the penal code in your state and protect yourself, your family, and your friends by obeying the law. This rulebook is not to be construed in any way as an aid to breaking the law. Its purpose is simply to maintain order by providing a fair framework for playing poker in a situation where the game is legal.

This rulebook for private games was made by taking the document constructed for cardroom use and making the appropriate changes. Most of those changes are in wording, but there are a few of substance. Here are some examples. A warning is given regarding the legality of hosting a poker game. The restriction on the maximum number of raises on a betting round was set at a bet and three raises for all limit poker forms, which is the traditional rule for private games. The procedure for shuffling and cutting is described. The time one may be gone from a game has been shortened.

TABLE OF CONTENTS

1.0: PROPER BEHAVIOR

1.1: CONDUCT CODE

We will attempt to maintain a pleasant environment for all our players, but are not responsible for the conduct of any player. We have established a code of conduct, and may deny the privilege to play in our game to anyone who violates it. The following is not permitted:

1. Collusion with another player or any other form of cheating.
2. Verbally or physically threatening anyone.
3. Using profanity or obscene language.
4. Creating a disturbance by arguing, shouting or making excessive noise.
5. Throwing, tearing, bending or crumpling cards.
6. Destroying or defacing property.
7. Using an illegal substance.
8. Carrying a weapon.

1.2: POKER ETIQUETTE

The following actions are improper, and grounds for warning, suspending or barring a violator:

1. Deliberately acting out of turn.
2. Deliberately splashing chips into the pot.
3. Agreeing to check a hand out when a third player is all-in.
4. Reading a hand for another player at the showdown before it has been placed face-up on the table.
5. Telling anyone to turn a hand face-up at the showdown.
6. Revealing the contents of a live hand in a multihanded pot before the betting is complete.
7. Needlessly stalling the action of a game.
8. Deliberately discarding hands away from the muck. Cards should be released in a low line of flight, at a moderate rate of speed.
9. Stacking chips in a manner that interferes with dealing or viewing cards.
10. Making statements or taking action that could unfairly influence the course of play, whether or not the offender is involved in the pot.

2.0: RUNNING THE GAME

2.1: DECISION-MAKING

1. Taking a seat in a poker game means you agree to abide by the rules for that game and the decision-making process used in it.
2. The proper time to draw attention to an error or irregularity is when it occurs or is first noticed. Any delay may affect the ruling.
3. If an incorrect rule interpretation or decision is made in good faith, there shall be no liability incurred by the decision-maker.
4. A ruling may be made regarding a pot if it has been requested before the next deal starts (or before the game either ends or changes to another table). Otherwise, the result of a deal must stand. The first riffle of the shuffle marks the start for a deal.
5. If a pot has been incorrectly awarded and mingled with chips that were not in the pot, but the time limit for a ruling request given in the previous rule has been complied with, the betting may be reconstructed, and the proper amount transferred to the respective players.
6. To keep the action moving, it is possible that a game may continue even though a decision is delayed for a short period. In such circumstances, a pot or portion thereof may be impounded while the decision is pending.
7. The same action may have a different meaning, depending on who does it, so the possible intent of an offender will be taken into consideration. Some factors here are the person's amount of poker experience and past record.

2.2: PROCEDURES

1. The poker form and stakes that had been agreed upon when the game was started shall not be changed if more than one player objects.
2. Cash is not permitted on the table. All cash should be changed into chips in order to play.
3. The establishment is not responsible for any shortage or removal of chips left on the table during a player's absence, even though everyone should try to protect the game as best they can.
4. All games are table stakes. Only the chips in front of a player at the start of a deal may play for that hand, except for chips not yet received

that a player has purchased. The amount bought must be announced to the table, or only the amount of the minimum buy-in plays.

5. If you return to the game within one hour of cashing out, your buy-in must be equal to the amount removed when leaving that game.

6. All chips must be kept in plain view.

7. Playing out of a chip rack is not allowed.

8. Only one person may play a hand.

9. No one is allowed to play another player's chips.

10. Playing over may be allowed if that is customary, but only with permission from the absent player (unless he has left the premises for some length of time) and protection for that person's chips.

11. Pushing bets ("saving" or "potting out") is not allowed.

12. Pushing an ante or posting for another person is not allowed.

13. Splitting pots by agreement will not be allowed. Chopping the big and small blind by taking them back when all other players have folded may be allowed in non-tournament button games, if that is customary.

14. Insurance propositions are not allowed. Dealing twice (or three times) when all-in is permitted at big-bet poker.

15. Players must keep their cards in full view. This means above table-level and not past the edge of the table. The cards should not be covered by the hands in a manner to completely conceal them.

16. Any player is entitled to a clear view of an opponent's chips. Higher denomination chips should be easily visible.

17. Your chips may be picked up if you are away from the table for more than 15 minutes, unless you have made a specific arrangement to leave for a longer length of time. Frequent absences may cause your chips to be removed from the table.

18. A new deck must be used for at least a full round (once around the table) before it may be changed, unless a deck is defective or damaged, or cards become sticky.

19. Looking through the discards or deck stub is not allowed.

20. A player is expected to pay attention to the game and not hold up play. Activity that interferes with this such as reading at the table is discouraged, and the player will be asked to cease if a problem is caused.

21. A non-player may not sit at the table.

22. You may have a guest sit behind you only if no one in the game objects. It is improper for a guest to look at any hand other then your own.
23. Speaking in a foreign language during a deal is not allowed.

2.3: SEATING

1. When a button game starts, active players will draw a card for the button position. The button will be awarded to the highest card by suit.
2. In starting a game, the player who arrives the earliest gets first choice of remaining seats. A certain seat may be reserved for a player for good reason. Example: to assist in ease of reading the board for a person with a vision problem.
3. A player who is already in the game has precedence over a new player for any seat when it becomes available. However, no change will occur after a new player has been seated and received chips. For players already in the game, the one who asks the earliest has preference for a seat change.

3.0: GENERAL POKER RULES

3.1: THE BUY-IN

1. When you enter a game, you must make a full buy-in for that particular game. A full buy-in at limit poker is at least ten times the maximum bet for the game being played, unless designated otherwise. A full buy-in at pot-limit or no-limit poker is forty times the minimum bring-in (usually, the size of the big blind), unless designated otherwise.
2. Only one short buy-in is allowed per session.
3. Adding to your stack is not considered a buy-in, and may be done in any quantity between hands.

3.2: THE SHUFFLE AND CUT

1. The pack must be shuffled and cut before the cards are dealt. The recommended method to protect the integrity of the game is to have three people involved instead of only two. The dealer on the previous hand takes in the discards and squares up the deck prior to the shuffle. The player on the new dealer's left shuffles the cards

and then slides the pack to the new dealer, who gets them cut by the player on his right.

2. The deck must be riffled a minimum of four times. The cut must leave a minimum of four cards in each portion.

3. The bottom of the deck should be protected so nobody can see the bottom card. This is done by using a cut-card. A joker may be used as a cut-card.

4. Any complaint about the shuffle, cut, or other preparation connected with dealing must be made before the player has looked at his hand or betting action has started.

3.3: MISDEALS

1. The following circumstances cause a misdeal, provided attention is called to the error before two players have acted on their hands. (If two players have acted in turn, the deal must be played to conclusion, as explained in rule #2)

   (a) The first or second card of the hand has been dealt face-up or exposed through dealer error.

   (b) Two or more cards have been exposed by the dealer.

   (c) Two or more boxed cards (improperly faced cards) are found.

   (d) Two or more extra cards have been dealt in the starting hands of a game.

   (e) An incorrect number of cards has been dealt to a player, except the top card may be dealt if it goes to the player in proper sequence.

   (f) Any card has been dealt out of the proper sequence (except an exposed card may be replaced by the burncard).

   (g) The button was out of position.

   (h) The first card was dealt to the wrong position.

   (i) Cards have been dealt to an empty seat or a player not entitled to a hand.

   (j) A player has been dealt out who is entitled to a hand. This player must be present at the table or have posted a blind or ante.

2. Action is considered to occur in stud games when two players after the forced bet have acted on their hands. In button games, action is considered to occur when two players after the blinds have acted on their hands. Once action occurs, a misdeal can no longer be declared. The hand will be played to conclusion and no money will be returned to any player whose hand is fouled.

3.4: DEAD HANDS

1. Your hand is declared dead if:

> (a) You fold or announce that you are folding when facing a bet or a raise.
>
> (b) You throw your hand away in a forward motion causing another player to act behind you (even if not facing a bet).
>
> (c) In stud, when facing a bet, you pick your upcards off the table, turn your upcards face-down, or mix your upcards and downcards together.
>
> (d) The hand does not contain the proper number of cards for that poker form (except at stud a hand missing the final card may be ruled live, and at lowball and draw high a hand with too few cards before the draw is live). [See 16.0: Explanations, discussion #4, for more information on the stud portion of this rule.]
>
> (e) You act on a hand with a joker as a holecard in a game not using a joker. (A player who acts on a hand without looking at a card assumes the liability of finding an improper card, as given in Irregularities, rule #8.)
>
> (f) You have the clock on you when facing a bet or raise and exceed the specified time limit.

2. Cards thrown into the muck may be ruled dead. However, a hand that is clearly identifiable may be retrieved if doing so is in the best interest of the game. An extra effort should be made to rule a hand retrievable if it was folded as a result of false information given to the player.

3. Cards thrown into another player's hand are dead, whether they are face-up or face-down.

3.5: IRREGULARITIES

1. In button games, if it is discovered that the button was placed incorrectly on the previous hand, the button and blinds will be corrected for the new hand in a manner that gives every player one chance for each position on the round (if possible).

2. You must protect your own hand at all times. Your cards may be protected with your hands, a chip or other object placed on top of them. If you fail to protect your hand, you will have no redress if it becomes fouled or the dealer accidentally kills it.

3. If a card with a different color back appears during a hand, all action is void and all chips in the pot are returned to the respective bettors. If a card with a different color back is discovered in the stub, all action stands.

4. If two cards of the same rank and suit are found, all action is void, and all chips in the pot are returned to the players who wagered them (subject to next rule).

5. A player who knows the deck is defective has an obligation to point this out. If such a player instead tries to win a pot by taking aggressive action (trying for a freeroll), the player may lose the right to a refund, and the chips may be required to stay in the pot for the next deal.

6. If there is extra money in the pot on a deal as a result of forfeited money from the previous deal (as per rule #5), or some similar reason, only a player dealt in on the previous deal is entitled to a hand.

7. A card discovered face-up in the deck (boxed card) will be treated as a meaningless scrap of paper. A card being treated as a scrap of paper will be replaced by the next card below it in the deck, except when the next card has already been dealt face-down to another player and mixed in with other downcards. In that case, the card that was face-up in the deck will be replaced after all other cards are dealt for that round.

8. A joker that appears in a game where it is not used is treated as a scrap of paper. Discovery of a joker does not cause a misdeal. If the joker is discovered before a player acts on his or her hand, it is replaced as in the previous rule. If the player does not call attention to the joker before acting, then the player has a dead hand.

9. If you play a hand without looking at all of your cards, you assume the liability of having an irregular card or an improper joker.

10. One or more cards missing from the deck does not invalidate the results of a hand.

11. Before the first round of betting, if a dealer deals one additional card, it is returned to the deck and used as the burncard.

12. Procedure for an exposed card varies with the poker form, and is given in the section for each game. A card that is flashed by a dealer is treated as an exposed card. A card that is flashed by a player will play. To obtain a ruling on whether a card was exposed

and should be replaced, a player should announce that the card was flashed or exposed before looking at it. A downcard dealt off the table is an exposed card.

13. If a card is exposed due to dealer error, a player does not have an option to take or reject the card. The situation will be governed by the rules for the particular game being played.

14. If you drop any cards out of your hand onto the floor, you must still play them.

15. If the dealer prematurely deals any cards before the betting is complete, those cards will not play, even if a player who has not acted decides to fold.

3.6: BETTING AND RAISING

1. Check-raise is permitted in all games, except in certain forms of lowball.

2. In no-limit and pot-limit games, unlimited raising is allowed.

3. In limit poker, for a pot involving three or more players who are not all-in, there is a maximum of a bet and three raises allowed.

4. Unlimited raising for money games is allowed in heads-up play. This applies any time the action becomes heads-up before the raising has been capped. Once the raising is capped on a betting round, it cannot be uncapped by a subsequent fold that leaves two players heads-up. For tournament play, the three raise maximum for limit poker applies when heads-up as well.

5. In limit play, an all-in wager of less than half a bet does not reopen the betting for any player who has already acted and is in the pot for all previous bets. A player facing less than half a bet may fold, call or complete the wager. An all-in wager of a half a bet or more is treated as a full bet, and a player may fold, call or make a full raise. (An example of a full raise is on a $20 betting round, raising a $15 all-in bet to $35).

6. Any wager must be at least the size of the previous bet or raise in that round, unless a player is going all-in.

7. The smallest chip that may be wagered in a game is the smallest chip used in the antes and/or blinds. Smaller chips than this do not play even in quantity, so a player wanting action on such chips must change them up between deals. If betting is in dollar units or

greater, a fraction of a dollar does not play. A player going all-in must put all chips that play into the pot.

8. A verbal statement denotes your action and is binding. If in turn you verbally declare a fold, check, bet, call or raise, you are forced to take that action.

9. Rapping the table with your hand is a pass.

10. Deliberately acting out of turn will not be tolerated. A player who checks out of turn may not bet or raise on the next turn to act. An action or verbal declaration out of turn may be ruled binding if there is no bet, call or raise by an intervening player acting after the infraction has been committed.

11. To retain the right to act, a player must stop the action by calling "time" (or an equivalent word). Failure to stop the action before three or more players have acted behind you may cause you to lose the right to act. You cannot forfeit your right to act if any player in front of you has not acted, only if you fail to act when it legally becomes your turn. Therefore, if you wait for someone whose turn comes before you, and three or more players act behind you, this still does not hinder your right to act.

12. A player who bets or calls by releasing chips into the pot is bound by that action. However, if you are unaware that the pot has been raised, you may withdraw that money and reconsider your action, provided that no one else has acted after you.

13. In limit poker, if you make a forward motion into the pot area with chips and thus cause another player to act, you may be forced to complete your action.

14. String raises are not allowed. To protect your right to raise, you should either declare your intention verbally or place the proper amount of chips into the pot. Putting a full bet plus a half-bet or more into the pot is considered to be the same as announcing a raise, and the raise must be completed. (This does not apply in the use of a single chip of greater value.)

15. If you put a single chip in the pot that is larger than the bet, but do not announce a raise, you are assumed to have only called. Example: In a $3-$6 game, when a player bets $6 and the next player puts a $25 chip in the pot without saying anything, that player has merely called the $6 bet.

16. All wagers and calls of an improperly low amount must be brought up to proper size if the error is discovered before the betting round has been completed. This includes actions such as betting a lower amount than the minimum bring-in (other than going all-in) and betting the lower limit on an upper limit betting round. If a wager is supposed to be made in a rounded off amount, is not, and must be corrected, it shall be changed to the proper amount nearest in size. No one who has acted may change a call to a raise because the wager size has been changed.

3.7: THE SHOWDOWN

1. A player must show all cards in the hand face-up on the table to win any part of the pot.
2. Cards speak (cards read for themselves). The dealer assists in reading hands, but players are responsible for holding onto their cards until the winner is declared. Although verbal declarations as to the contents of a hand are not binding, deliberately miscalling a hand with the intent of causing another player to discard a winning hand is unethical and may result in forfeiture of the pot. (For more information on miscalling a hand see 11.0: Lowball, Rule 15 and Rule 16.)
3. Anyone who sees an incorrect amount of chips put into the pot, or an error about to be made in awarding a pot, has an ethical obligation to point out the error. Please help us keep mistakes of this nature to a minimum.
4. All losing hands will be killed by the dealer before a pot is awarded.
5. Any player who has been dealt in may request to see any hand that has been called, even if the opponent's hand or the winning hand has been mucked. However, this is a privilege that may be revoked if abused. If a player other than the pot winner asks to see a hand that has been folded, that hand is dead. If the winning player asks to see a losing player's hand, both hands are live, and the best hand wins.
6. If you show cards to another player during or after a deal, any player at the table has the right to see those exposed cards. Cards shown during a deal to a player not in the pot should only be shown to all players when the deal is finished.

7. If everyone checks (or is all-in) on the final betting round, the player who acted first is the first to show the hand. If there is wagering on the final betting round, the last player to take aggressive action by a bet or raise is the first to show the hand. In order to speed up the game, a player holding a probable winner is encouraged to show the hand without delay. If there is a side pot, players involved in the side pot should show their hands before anyone who is all-in for only the main pot.

3.8: TIES

1. The ranking of suits from highest to lowest is spades, hearts, diamonds, clubs. Suits never break a tie for winning a pot. Suits are used to break a tie between cards of the same rank (no redeal or redraw).
2. Dealing a card to each player is used to determine things like who moves to another table. If the cards are dealt, the order is clockwise starting with the first player on the dealer's left (the button position is irrelevant). Drawing a card is used to determine things like who gets the button in a new game.
3. An odd chip will be broken down to the smallest unit used in the game.
4. No player may receive more than one odd chip.
5. If two or more hands tie, an odd chip will be awarded as follows:
   (a) In a button game, the first hand clockwise from the button gets the odd chip.
   (b) In a stud game, the odd chip will be given to the highest card by suit in all high games, and to the lowest card by suit in all low games. (When making this determination, all cards are used, not just the five cards that constitute the player's hand.)
   (c) In high-low split games, the high hand receives the odd chip in a split between the high and the low hands. The odd chip between tied high hands is awarded as in a high game of that poker form, and the odd chip between tied low hands is awarded as in a low game of that poker form.
   (d) All side pots and the main pot will be split as separate pots, not mixed together.

4.0: BUTTON AND BLIND USE

In button games, If the players deal the cards themselves, "the button" refers to the person who dealt the cards. (If a non-playing dealer does the actual dealing, a round disk called the button is used to indicate which player has the dealer position.) The player with the button is last to receive cards on the initial deal and has the right of last action after the first betting round. The button moves clockwise after a deal ends to rotate the advantage of last action. One or more blind bets are usually used to stimulate action and initiate play. Blinds are posted before the players look at their cards. Blinds are part of a player's bet, unless the structure of a game or the situation requires part or all of a particular blind to be "dead." Dead chips are not part of a player's bet. With two blinds, the small blind is posted by the player immediately clockwise from the button, and the big blind is posted by the player two positions clockwise from the button. With more than two blinds, the little blind is normally left of the button (not on it). Action is initiated on the first betting round by the first player to the left of the blinds. On all subsequent betting rounds, the action begins with the first active player to the left of the button.

RULES FOR USING BLINDS

1. Each round every player must get an opportunity for the button, and meet the total amount of the blind obligations. Either of the following methods of button and blind placement may be designated to do this:
    (a) Moving button – The button always moves forward to the next player and the blinds adjust accordingly. There may be more than one big blind.
    (b) Dead button – The big blind is posted by the player due for it, and the small blind and button are positioned accordingly, even if this means the small blind or the button is placed in front of an empty seat, giving the same player the privilege of last action on consecutive hands. [See 16.0: Explanations, discussion #1, for more information on this rule.]
2. A player who posts a blind has the option of raising the pot at the first turn to act. (This does not apply when a "dead blind" for the collection is used in a game and has been posted).

3. In heads-up play with two blinds, the small blind is on the button.
4. A new player entering the game has the following options:
   (a) Wait for the big blind.
   (b) Post an amount equal to the big blind and immediately be dealt a hand. (In lowball, a new player must either post an amount double the big blind or wait for the big blind.)
5. A new player who elects to let the button go by once without posting is not treated as a player in the game who has missed a blind, and needs to post only the big blind when entering the game.
6. A person playing over is considered a new player, and must post the amount of the big blind or wait for the big blind.
7. A new player cannot be dealt in between the big blind and the button. Blinds may not be made up between the big blind and the button. You must wait until the button passes. [See 16.0: Explanations, discussion #3, for more information on this rule.]
8. When you post the big blind, it serves as your opening bet. When it is your next turn to act, you have the option to raise.
9. A player who misses any or all blinds can resume play by either posting all the blinds missed or waiting for the big blind. If you choose to post the total amount of the blinds, an amount up to the size of the minimum opening bet is live. The remainder is taken by the dealer to the center of the pot and is not part of your bet. When it is your next turn to act, you have the option to raise.
10. If a player who owes a blind (as a result of a missed blind) is dealt in without posting, the hand is dead if the player looks at it before putting up the required chips, and has not yet acted. If the player acts on the hand and plays it, putting chips into the pot before the error is discovered, the hand is live, and the player is required to post on the next deal.
11. A player who goes all-in and loses is obligated to make up the blinds if they are missed before a rebuy is made. (The person is not treated as a new player when reentering.)
12. These rules about blinds apply to a newly started game:
    (a) Any player who drew for the button is considered active in the game and is required to make up any missed blinds.
    (b) A new player will not be required to post a blind until the button has made one complete revolution around the table, provided a blind has not yet passed that seat.

(c) A player may change seats without penalty, provided a blind has not yet passed the new seat.

13. In all multiple-blind games, a player who changes seats will be dealt in on the first available hand in the same relative position. Example: If you move two active positions away from the big blind, you must wait two hands before being dealt in again. If you move closer to the big blind, you can be dealt in without any penalty. If you do not wish to wait and have not yet missed a blind, then you can post an amount equal to the big blind and receive a hand. (Exception: At lowball you must kill the pot, wait for the same relative position, or wait for the big blind; see 11.0: Lowball, rule #7.)

14. A player who "deals off" (by playing the button and then immediately getting up to change seats) can allow the blinds to pass the new seat one time and reenter the game behind the button without having to post a blind.

15. A live "straddle bet" is not allowed at limit poker except in specified games.

5.0: HOLD 'EM

In hold 'em, players receive two downcards as their personal hand (holecards), after which there is a round of betting. Three boardcards are turned simultaneously (called the "flop") and another round of betting occurs. The next two boardcards are turned one at a time, with a round of betting after each card. The boardcards are community cards, and a player may use any five-card combination from among the board and personal cards. A player may even use all of the boardcards and no personal cards to form a hand (play the board). A dealer button is used. The usual structure is to use two blinds, but it is possible to play the game with one blind, multiple blinds, an ante, or combination of blinds plus an ante.

RULES

These rules deal only with irregularities. See the previous chapter, "Button and Blind Use," for rules on that subject.

1. If the first holecard dealt is exposed, a misdeal results. The dealer will retrieve the card, reshuffle, and recut the cards. If any other holecard is exposed due to a dealer error, the deal continues. The exposed card may not be kept. After completing the hand, the dealer replaces the card with the top card on the deck, and the exposed card is then used for the burncard. If more than one holecard is exposed, this is a misdeal and there must be a redeal.

2. If the flop contains too many cards, it must be redealt. (This applies even if it were possible to know which card was the extra one.)

3. If the flop needs to be redealt because the cards were prematurely flopped before the betting was complete, or the flop contained too many cards, the boardcards are mixed with the remainder of the deck. The burncard remains on the table. After shuffling, the dealer cuts the deck and deals a new flop without burning a card. [See 16.0: Explanations, discussion #2, for more information on this rule.]

4. If the dealer turns the fourth card on the board before the betting round is complete, the card is taken out of play for that round, even if subsequent players elect to fold. The betting is then completed. The dealer burns and turns what would have been the fifth card in the fourth card's place. After this round of betting, the dealer reshuffles the deck, including the card that was taken out of play, but not including the burncards or discards. The dealer then cuts the deck and turns the final card without burning a card. If the fifth card is turned up prematurely, the deck is reshuffled and dealt in the same manner. [See 16.0: Explanations, discussion #2, for more information on this rule.]

5. If the dealer mistakenly deals the first player an extra card (after all players have received their starting hands), the card will be returned to the deck and used for the burncard. If the dealer mistakenly deals more than one extra card, it is a misdeal.

6. You must declare that you are playing the board before you throw your cards away; otherwise you relinquish all claim to the pot.

6.0: OMAHA

Omaha is similar to hold 'em in using a three-card flop on the board, a fourth boardcard, and then a fifth boardcard. Each player is dealt four holecards (instead of two) at the start. In order to make a hand, a player must use precisely two holecards with three boardcards. The betting is the same as in hold 'em. At the showdown, the entire four-card hand should be shown to receive the pot.

RULES OF OMAHA

1. All the rules of hold 'em apply to Omaha except the rule on playing the board, which is not possible in Omaha (because you must use two cards from your hand and three cards from the board).

7.0: OMAHA HIGH-LOW

Omaha is often played high-low split, 8-or-better. The player may use any combination of two holecards and three boardcards for the high hand and another (or the same) combination of two holecards and three boardcards for the low hand.

The rules governing kill pots are listed in 13.0: Kill Pots.

RULES OF OMAHA HIGH-LOW

1. All the rules of Omaha apply to Omaha high-low split except as below.
2. A qualifier of 8-or-better for low applies to all high-low split games, unless a specific posting to the contrary is displayed. If there is no qualifying hand for low, the best high hand wins the whole pot.

8.0: SEVEN-CARD STUD

Seven-card stud is played with two downcards and one upcard dealt before the first betting round, followed by three more upcards (with a betting round after each card). After the last downcard is dealt, there is a final round of betting. The best five-card poker hand wins the pot. In all fixed-limit games, the smaller bet is wagered on the first two betting rounds, and the larger bet is wagered after the betting rounds on the fifth, sixth and seventh cards. If there is an open pair on the fourth card, any player has the option of making the smaller or larger bet. Deliberately changing the order of your upcards in a stud game is improper because it unfairly misleads the other players.

RULES OF SEVEN-CARD STUD

1. The first round of betting starts with a forced bet by the lowest upcard by suit. On subsequent betting rounds, the high hand on board initiates the action (a tie is broken by position, with the player who received cards first acting first).
2. The player with the forced bet has the option of opening for a full bet.
3. Increasing the amount wagered by the opening forced bet up to a full bet does not count as a raise, but merely as a completion of the bet. For example: In $15-$30 stud, the lowcard opens for $5. If the next player increases the bet to $15 (completes the bet), up to three raises are then allowed when using a three-raise limit.
4. In all fixed-limit games, when an open pair is showing on fourth street (second upcard), any player has the option of betting either the lower or the upper limit. For example: In a $5-$10 game, if you have a pair showing and are the high hand, you may bet either $5 or $10. If you bet $5, any player then has the option to call $5, raise $5, or raise $10. If a $10 raise is made, then all other raises must be in increments of $10. If the player high with the open pair on fourth street checks, then subsequent players have the same options that were given to the player who was high.
5. If your first or second holecard is accidentally turned up by the dealer, then your third card will be dealt down. If both holecards are dealt up, you have a dead hand and receive your ante back. If the first card dealt face-up would have been the lowcard, action starts with the first hand to that player's left. That player may fold, open for

the forced bet, or open for a full bet. (In tournament play, if a downcard is dealt face-up, a misdeal is called.)

6. If you are not present at the table when it is your turn to act on your hand, you forfeit your ante and your forced bet, if any. If you have not returned to the table in time to act, the hand will be killed when the betting reaches your seat.

7. If a hand is folded when there is no wager, that seat will continue to receive cards until the hand is killed as a result of a bet.

8. If you are all in for the ante and have the lowcard, the player to your left acts first. That player may fold, open for the forced bet, or open for a full bet.

9. If the wrong person is designated as low and that person bets, the action will be corrected to the true lowcard if the next player has not yet acted. The incorrect lowcard takes back the wager and the true lowcard must bet. If the next hand has acted after the incorrect lowcard wager, the wager stands, action continues from there, and the true lowcard has no obligations.

10. If you pick up your upcards without calling when facing a wager, this is a fold and your hand is dead. This act has no significance at the showdown because betting is over; the hand is live until discarded.

11. A card dealt off the table must play and it is treated as an exposed card.

12. Dealers should not announce possible straights or flushes.

13. If the dealer burns two cards for one round or fails to burn a card, the cards will be corrected, if at all possible, to their proper positions. If this should happen on a final downcard, and either a card intermingles with a player's other holecards or a player looks at the card, the player must accept that card.

14. If the dealer burns and deals one or more cards before a round of betting has been completed, the card(s) must be eliminated from play. After the betting for that round is completed, an additional card for each remaining player still active in the hand is also eliminated from play (to later deal the same cards to the players who would have received them without the error). After that round of betting has concluded, the dealer burns a card and play resumes. The removed cards are held off to the side in the event the dealer runs out of cards. If the prematurely dealt card is the final downcard and has been looked at or intermingled with the player's other holecards, the player must keep the card, and on

sixth street betting may not bet or raise (because the player now has all seven cards).

15. If there are not enough cards left in the deck for all players, all the cards are dealt except the last card, which is mixed with the burncards (and any cards removed from the deck, as in the previous rule). The dealer then scrambles and cuts these cards, burns again, and delivers the remaining downcards, using the last card if necessary. If there are not as many cards as players remaining without a card, the dealer does not burn, so that each player can receive a fresh card. If the dealer determines that there will not be enough fresh cards for all of the remaining players, then the dealer announces to the table that a common card will be used. The dealer will burn a card and turn one card face-up in the center of the table as a common card that plays in everyone's hand. The player who is now high using the common card initiates the action for the last round.

16. An all-in player should receive holecards dealt face-down, but if the final holecard to such a player is dealt face-up, the card must be kept, and the other players receive their normal card.

17. If the dealer turns the last card face-up to any player, the hand now high on the board using all the upcards will start the action. The following rules apply to the dealing of cards:

    (a) If there are more than two players, all remaining players receive their last card face-down. A player whose last card is face-up has the option of declaring all-in (before betting action starts).

    (b) If there are only two players remaining and the first player's final downcard is dealt face-up, the second player's final downcard will also be dealt face-up, and the betting proceeds as normal. In the event the first player's final card is dealt face-down and the opponent's final card is dealt face-up, the player with the face-up final card has the option of declaring all-in (before betting action starts).

18. A hand with more than seven cards is dead. A hand with less than seven cards at the showdown is dead, except any player missing a seventh card may have the hand ruled live. [See 16.0: Explanations, discussion #4, for more information on this rule.]

19. A player who calls a bet even though beaten by an opponent's upcards is not entitled to a refund. (The player is receiving information about an opponent's hand that is not available for free.)

9.0: SEVEN-CARD STUD LOW (RAZZ)

The lowest hand wins the pot. The format is similar to seven-card stud high, except the high card (aces are low) is required to make the forced bet on the first round, and the low hand acts first on all subsequent rounds. Straights and flushes have no ranking, so the best possible hand is 5-4-3-2-A (a wheel). An open pair does not affect the betting limit.

RULES OF RAZZ

1. All seven-card stud rules apply in razz except as otherwise noted.

2. The lowest hand wins the pot. Aces are low, and straights and flushes have no effect on the low value of a hand. The best possible hand is 5-4-3-2-A.

3. The highest card by suit starts the action with a forced bet. The low hand acts first on all subsequent rounds. If the low hand is tied, the first player clockwise from the dealer starts the action.

4. Fixed-limit games use the lower limit on third and fourth streets and the upper limit on subsequent streets. An open pair does not affect the limit.

10.0: SEVEN-CARD STUD HIGH-LOW

Seven-card stud high-low split is a stud game which is played both high and low. A qualifier of 8-or-better for low applies to all high-low split games, unless a specific posting to the contrary is displayed. The low card initiates the action on the first round, with an ace counting as a high card for this purpose. On subsequent rounds, the high hand initiates the action. If the high hand is tied, the first player clockwise from the dealer acts first. Fixed-limit games use the lower limit on third and fourth street and the upper limit on subsequent betting rounds, and an open pair does not affect the limit. Aces may be used for high or low. Straights and flushes do not affect the low value of a hand. A player may use any five cards to make the best high hand, and the same or any other grouping of five cards to make the best low hand.

RULES OF SEVEN-CARD STUD HIGH-LOW

1. All rules for seven-card stud apply to seven-card stud high-low split, except as otherwise noted.

2. A qualifier of 8-or-better for low applies to all high-low split games, unless a specific posting to the contrary is displayed. If there is no qualifying hand for low, the best high hand wins the whole pot.

3. A player may use any five cards to make the best high hand and any five cards, whether the same as the high hand or not, to make the best low hand.

4. The low card by suit initiates the action on the first round, with an ace counting as a high card for this purpose.

5. An ace may be used for high or low.

6. Straights and flushes do not affect the value of a low hand.

7. Fixed-limit games use the lower limit on third and fourth streets and the upper limit on subsequent rounds. An open pair on fourth street does not affect the limit.

8. Splitting pots is only determined by the cards and not by agreement among players.

9. When there is an odd chip in a pot, the chip goes to the high hand. If two players split the pot by tying for both the high and the low, the pot shall be split as evenly as possible, and the player with the highest card by suit receives the odd chip. When making this determination, all cards are used, not just the five cards used for the final hand played.

10. When there is one odd chip in the high portion of the pot and two or more high hands split all or half the pot, the odd chip goes to the player with the high card by suit. When two or more low hands split half the pot, the odd chip goes to the player with the low card by suit.

11.0: LOWBALL

Lowball is draw poker with the lowest hand winning the pot. Each player is dealt five cards face-down, after which there is a betting round. Players are required to open with a bet or fold. The players who remain in the pot after the first betting round now have an option to improve their hand by replacing cards in their hands with new ones. This is the draw. The game is normally played with one or more blinds, sometimes with an ante added. Some betting structures allow the big blind to be called; other structures require the minimum open to be double the big blind. In limit poker, the usual structure has the limit double after the draw (Northern California is an exception). The most popular forms of lowball are ace-to-five lowball (also known as California lowball), and deuce-to-seven lowball (also known as Kansas City lowball). Ace-to-five lowball gets its name because the best hand at that form is 5-4-3-2-A. Deuce-to-seven lowball gets its name because the best hand at that form is 7-5-4-3-2 (not of the same suit). For a further description of the forms of lowball, please see the individual section for each game. All rules governing kill pots are listed in 13.0: Kill Pots.

RULES OF LOWBALL

1. The rules governing misdeals for hold 'em and other button games will be used for lowball. [See 16.0 Explanations, discussion #7, for more information on this rule.] These rules governing misdeals are reprinted here for convenience.

   "The following circumstances cause a misdeal, provided attention is called to the error before two players have acted on their hands:

   (a) The first or second card of the hand has been dealt face-up or exposed through dealer error.

   (b) Two or more cards have been exposed by the dealer.

   (c) Two or more extra cards have been dealt in the starting hands of a game.

   (d) An incorrect number of cards has been dealt to a player, except the button may receive one more card to complete a starting hand.

   (e) The button was out of position.

   (f) The first card was dealt to the wrong position.

   (g) Cards have been dealt out of the proper sequence.

(h) Cards have been dealt to an empty seat or a player not entitled to a hand.

(i) A player has been dealt out who is entitled to a hand. This player must be present at the table or have posted a blind or ante."

2. As a new player, you have two options:

(a) To wait for the big blind.

(b) To kill the pot for double the amount of the big blind.

3. In a single-blind game, a player who has less than half a blind may receive a hand. However, the next player is obligated to take the blind. If the all-in player wins the pot or buys in again, that player will then be obligated to either take the blind on the next deal or sit out until due for the big blind.

4. In single-blind games, half a blind or more constitutes a full blind.

5. In single-blind games, if you fail to take the blind, you may only be dealt in on the blind.

6. In multiple-blind games, if for any reason the big blind passes your seat, you may either wait for the big blind or kill the pot in order to receive a hand. This does not apply if you have taken all of your blinds and changed seats. In this situation, you may be dealt in as soon as your position relative to the blinds entitles you to a hand (the button may go by you once without penalty).

7. Before the draw, whether an exposed card must be taken depends on the form of lowball being played; see that form. (The player never has an option.)

8. On the draw, an exposed card cannot be taken. The draw is completed to each player in order, and then the exposed card is replaced.

9. A player may draw up to four consecutive cards. If a player wishes to draw five new cards, four are dealt right away, and the fifth card after everyone else has drawn cards. If the last player wishes to draw five new cards, four are dealt right away, and a card is burned before the player receives a fifth card. [See 16.0: Explanations, discussion #9, for more information about this rule.]

10. Five cards constitute a playing hand; more or fewer than five cards after the draw constitutes a fouled hand. Before the draw, if you have fewer than five cards in your hand, you may receive additional cards, provided no action has been taken by the first player to act (unless that action occurs before the deal is completed). However,

the dealer position may still receive a missing fifth card, even if action has taken place. If action has been taken, you are entitled on the draw to receive the number of cards necessary to complete a five-card hand.

11. You may change the number of cards you wish to draw, provided:
   (a) No card has been dealt off the deck in response to your request (including the burncard).
   (b) No player has acted, in either the betting or indicating the number of cards to be drawn, based on the number of cards you have requested.

12. If you are asked how many cards you drew by another active player, you are obligated to respond until there has been action after the draw, and the dealer is also obligated to respond. Once there is any action after the draw, you are no longer obliged to respond and the dealer cannot respond.

13. Rapping the table in turn constitutes either a pass or the declaration of a pat hand that does not want to draw any cards, depending on the situation.

14. Cards speak (cards read for themselves). However, you are not allowed to claim a better hand than you hold. (Example: If a player calls an "8", that player must produce at least an "8" low or better to win. But if a player erroneously calls the second card incorrectly, such as "8-6" when actually holding an 8-7, no penalty applies.) If you miscall your hand and cause another player to foul his or her hand, your hand is dead. If both hands remain intact, the best hand wins. If a miscalled hand occurs in a multihanded pot, the miscalled hand is dead, and the best remaining hand wins the pot. For your own protection, always hold your hand until you see your opponent's cards.

16. Any player spreading a hand with a pair in it must announce "pair" or risk losing the pot if it causes any other player to foul a hand. If two or more hands remain intact, the best hand wins the pot.

11.1: ACE-TO-FIVE LOWBALL

In ace-to-five lowball, the best hand is any 5-4-3-2-A. Straights and flushes do not count against your hand.

1. If a joker is used, it becomes the lowest card not present in your hand. The joker is assumed to be in use unless the contrary is posted.

2. In limit play, check-raise is not permitted (unless the players are alerted that it is allowed).

3. In limit ace-to-five lowball, before the draw, an exposed card of seven or under must be taken, and an exposed card higher than a seven must be replaced after the deal has been completed. This first exposed card is used as the burncard. [See 16.0: Explanations, discussion #8, for more information on this rule.]

4. Some lowball games may wish to employ the "sevens rule." It works as follows. If you check a seven or better and it is the best hand, all action after the draw is void, and you cannot win any money on any subsequent bets. You are still eligible to win whatever existed in the pot before the draw if you have the best hand. If you check a seven or better and the hand is beaten, you lose the pot and any additional calls you make. If there is an all-in bet after the draw that is less than half a bet, a seven or better may just call and win that bet. However, if another player overcalls this short bet and loses, the person who overcalls receives the bet back. If the seven or better completes to a full bet, this fulfills all obligations.

11.2: DEUCE-TO-SEVEN LOWBALL

In deuce-to-seven lowball (sometimes known as Kansas City lowball), in most respects, the worst conventional poker hand wins. Straights and flushes count against you, crippling the value of a hand. The ace is used only as a high card. Therefore, the best hand is 7-5-4-3-2, not all of the same suit. The hand 5-4-3-2-A is not considered to be a straight, but an ace-5 high, so it beats other ace-high hands and pairs, but loses to king-high. A pair of aces is the highest pair, so it loses to any other pair.

The rules for deuce-to-seven lowball are the same as those for ace-to-five lowball, except for the following differences:

1. The best hand is 7-5-4-3-2 of at least two different suits. Straights and flushes count against you, and aces are considered high only.

2. Before the draw, an exposed card of 7, 5, 4, 3, or 2 must be taken. Any other exposed card must be replaced (including a 6).

3. Check-raise is allowed on any hand after the draw, and a seven or better is not required to bet.

11.3: NO-LIMIT AND POT-LIMIT LOWBALL

1. All the rules for no-limit and pot-limit poker (see 14.0: No-Limit and Pot-Limit) apply to no-limit and pot-limit lowball. All other lowball rules apply, except as noted.

    A player is not entitled to know that an opponent does not hold the best possible hand, so these rules for exposed cards before the draw apply:

    (a) In ace-to-five lowball, a player must take an exposed card of A, 2, 3, 4, or 5, and any other card must be replaced.

    (b) In deuce-to-seven lowball, the player must take an exposed card of 2, 3, 4, 5, or 7, and any other card including a 6 must be replaced.

    After the draw, any exposed card must be replaced.

4. After the draw, a player may check any hand without penalty (The sevens rule is not used).

5. Check-raise is allowed.

12.0: DRAW HIGH

There are two betting rounds, one before the draw and one after the draw. The game is played with a button and an ante. Players in turn may check, open for the minimum, or open with a raise. After the first betting round the players have the opportunity to draw new cards to replace the ones they discard. Action after the draw starts with the opener, or next player proceeding clockwise if the opener has folded. The betting limit after the draw is twice the amount of the betting limit before the draw. Some draw high games allow a player to open on anything; others require the opener to have a pair of jacks or better.

RULES OF DRAW HIGH

1. A maximum of a bet and four raises is permitted in multihanded pots. [See 16.0: Explanations, discussion #6, for more information on this rule.]

2. Check-raise is permitted both before and after the draw.

3. Any card that is exposed by the dealer before the draw must be kept.

4. Five cards constitute a playing hand. Less than five cards for a player (other than the button) before action has been taken is a misdeal. If action has been taken, a player with fewer than five cards may draw the number of cards necessary to complete a five-card hand. The button may receive the fifth card even if action has taken place. More or fewer than five cards after the draw constitutes a fouled hand.

5. A player may draw up to four consecutive cards. If a player wishes to draw five new cards, four are dealt right away, and the fifth card after everyone else has drawn cards. If the last player wishes to draw five new cards, four are dealt right away, and a card is burned before the player receives a fifth card. [See 16.0: Explanations, discussion #9, for more information about this rule.]

6. You may change the number of cards you wish to draw, provided:
   (a) No cards have been dealt off the deck in response to your request (including the burncard).
   (b) No player has acted, in either the betting or indicating the number of cards to be drawn, based on the number of cards you have requested.

7. If you are asked how many cards you drew by another active player, you are obligated to respond until there has been action after the draw, and the dealer is also obligated to respond. Once there is any action after the draw, you are no longer obliged to respond and the dealer cannot respond.

8. On the draw, an exposed card cannot be taken. The draw is completed to each player in order, and then the exposed card is replaced.

9. Rapping the table in turn constitutes either a pass or the declaration of a pat hand that does not want to draw any cards, depending on the situation. A player who indicates a pat hand by rapping the table, not knowing the pot has been raised, may still play his or her hand.

10. You may not change your seat between hands when there are multiple antes or forfeited money in the pot.

11. You have the right to pay the ante (whether single or multiple) at any time and receive a hand, unless there is any additional money in the pot that has been forfeited during a hand in which you were not involved.

12. If the pot has been declared open by an all-in player playing for just the antes, all callers must come in for the full opening bet.

13. If you have only a full ante and no other chips on the table, you may play for just the antes. If no one opens and there is another ante, you may still play for that part of the antes that you have matched, without putting in any more money.

12.1: JACKS-OR-BETTER

1. A pair of jacks or better is required to open the pot. If no player opens the pot, the button moves forward and each player must ante again, unless the limit of antes has been reached for that particular game. (Most games allow three consecutive deals before anteing stops.)

2. If the opener should show false openers before the draw, any other active player has the opportunity to declare the pot opened. However, any player who originally passed openers is not eligible to declare the pot open. The false opener has a dead hand and the opening bet stays in the pot. Any other bet placed in the pot by the opener may be withdrawn, provided the action before the draw is not completed. If no other player declares the pot open, all bets are returned except the opener's first bet. The first bet and antes will remain in the pot, and all players who were involved in that hand are entitled to play the next hand after anteing again.

3. Any player who has legally declared the pot opened must prove openers in order to win the pot.

4. In all cases, the pot will play (even if the opener shows or declares a fouled hand) if there has been a raise, two or more players call the opening bet, or all action is completed before the draw.

5. Even if you are all in for just the ante (or part of the ante), you may declare the pot open if you have openers. If you are all in and falsely declare the pot open, you will lose the ante money and may not continue to play on any subsequent deals until a winner is determined. Even if you buy in again, you must wait until the pot has been legally opened and someone else has won it before you can resume playing.

6. Once action has been completed before the draw, the opener may not withdraw any bets, whether or not the hand contains openers.

7. An opener may be allowed to retrieve a discarded hand to prove openers, at management's discretion.

8. Any player may request that the opener retain the opening hand and show it after the winner of the pot has been determined.

9. You may split openers, but you must declare that you are splitting and place all discards under a chip to be exposed by the dealer after the completion of the hand. If you declare that you are splitting openers, but it is determined that you could not possibly have had openers when your final hand is compared with your discards, you will lose the pot.

10. You are not splitting openers if you retain openers. If you begin with the ace, joker, king, queen of spades, and the ten of clubs, you are not splitting if you throw the ten of clubs away. You are breaking a straight to draw to a royal flush, and in doing so, you have retained openers (ace-joker for two aces).

11. After the draw, if you call the opener's bet and cannot beat openers, you will not get your bet back. (You have received information about opener's hand that is not free.)

12.2: THE JOKER

1. The players will be alerted as to whether the joker is in use.

2. The joker may be used only as an ace, or to complete a straight, flush, or straight flush. (Thus it is not a completely wild card.)

3. If the joker is used to make a flush, it will be the highest card of the flush not present in the hand.

4. Five aces is the best possible hand (four aces and joker).

13.0: KILL POTS

To kill a pot means to post an overblind that increases the betting limit. A full kill is double the amount of the big blind, and doubles the betting limits. A half kill is one-and-a-half times the big blind, and increases the betting limits by that amount. A kill may be optional in a game, and is often used at lowball when a player wants to be dealt in right away instead of waiting to take the big blind. A kill may be required in a game for any time a specified event takes place. In high-low split games using a required kill, a player who scoops a pot bigger than a set size must kill the next pot. In other games using a required kill, a player who wins two consecutive pots must kill the next pot. In this type of kill game, a marker called a "kill button" indicates which player has won the pot, and the winner keeps this marker until the next hand is completed. If the player who has the kill button wins a second consecutive pot and it qualifies monetarily, that player must kill the next pot.

RULES OF KILL POTS

1. The kill button is neutral (belonging to no player) if:
    (a) It is the first hand of a new game.
    (b) The winner of the previous pot has quit the game.
    (c) The previous pot was split and neither player had the kill button.
2. In a kill pot, the killer acts in proper turn (after the person on the immediate right).
3. There is no pot-size requirement for the first pot or "leg" of a kill. For the second "leg" to qualify for a kill, you must win at least one full bet for whatever limit you are playing, and it cannot be any part of the blind structure.
4. If a player with one "leg up" splits the next pot, that player still has a "leg up" for the next hand. If the player who split the pot was the kill in the previous hand, then that player must also kill the next pot.
5. A person who leaves the table with a "leg up" toward a kill still has a "leg up" upon returning to the game.
6. A player who is required to post a kill must do so that same hand even if wishing to quit or be dealt out. A player who fails to post a required kill blind will not be allowed to participate in any game until the kill money is posted.
7. Kill blinds are considered part of the pot. If a player with a required kill wins again, then that player must kill it again (for the same amount as the previous hand).
8. When a player wins both the high and the low pot ("scoops") in a split-pot game with a kill provision, the next hand will be killed only if the pot is at least five times the size of the upper limit of the game.
9. If you are unaware that the pot has been killed and put in a lesser amount, if it is a required kill pot with the kill button face-up, you must put in the correct amount. If not, you may withdraw the chips and reconsider your action.

10. In lowball, an optional rule is allowing players to look at their first two cards and then opt whether to kill the pot. The pot may no longer be killed if any player in the game has received a third card. In order to kill the pot voluntarily, you must have at least four times the amount of the kill blind in your stack. For example: If the big blind is two chips, and the kill blind is four chips, the voluntary killer must have at least 16 chips prior to posting the kill. If this rule is used, it is in conjunction with having the killer act last on the first betting round rather than in proper order.
11. Only one kill is allowed per deal.
12. A new player is not entitled to play in a killed pot, but may do so by agreeing to kill the next pot.
13. Broken game status is allowed only for players of the same limit and game type. For this purpose, a game with a required kill is considered a different type of game than an otherwise similar game without a required kill.

14.0: NO LIMIT AND POT-LIMIT

A no-limit or pot-limit betting structure for a game gives it a different character from limit poker, requiring a separate set of rules in many situations. All the rules for limit games apply to no-limit and pot-limit games, except as noted in this section. No-limit means that the amount of a wager is limited only by the table stakes rule, so any part or all of a player's chips may be wagered. The rules of no-limit play also apply to pot-limit play, except that a bet may not exceed the pot size. For those rules that apply only to no-limit and pot-limit lowball, see the subsection at the end of 11.0: Lowball.

14.1: NO-LIMIT RULES
1. The number of raises in any betting round is not limited.
2. All bets must be at least equal to the minimum bring-in, unless the player is going all-in. (A straddle bet sets a new minimum bring-in, and is not treated as a raise.)
3. All raises must be equal to or greater than the size of the previous bet or raise on that betting round, except for an all-in wager. A

player who has already checked or called may not subsequently raise an all-in bet that is less than the full size of the last bet or raise. (The half-the-size rule for reopening the betting is for limit poker only.)

> Example: Player A bets $100 and Player B raises $100 more, making the total bet $200. If Player C goes all in for less than $300 total (not a full $100 raise), and Player A calls, then Player B has no option to raise again, because he wasn't fully raised. (Player A could have raised, because Player B raised.)

4. A wager is not binding until the chips are actually released into the pot, unless the player has made a verbal statement of action.

5. If there is a discrepancy between a player's verbal statement and the amount put into the pot, the bet will be corrected to the verbal statement.

6. If a call is short due to a counting error, the amount must be corrected, even if the bettor has shown down a superior hand.

7. Because the amount of a wager at big-bet poker has such a wide range, a player who has taken action based on a gross misunderstanding of the amount wagered needs some protection. A bettor should not show down a hand until the amount put into the pot for a call seems reasonably correct, or it is obvious that the caller understands the amount wagered. The decision-maker is allowed considerable discretion in ruling on this type of situation. A possible rule-of-thumb is to disallow any claim of not understanding the amount wagered if the caller has put eighty percent or more of that amount into the pot.

> Example: On the end, a player puts a $500 chip into the pot and says softly, "Four hundred." The opponent puts a $100 chip into the pot and says, "Call." The bettor immediately shows the hand. The dealer says, "He bet four hundred." The caller says, "Oh, I thought he bet a hundred." In this case, the recommended ruling normally is that the bettor had an obligation to not show the hand when the amount put into the pot was obviously short, and the "call" can be retracted. Note that the character of each player can be a factor. (Unfortunately, situations can arise at big-bet poker that are not so clear-cut as this.)

8. A player who says "raise" is allowed to continue putting chips into the pot with more than one move; the wager is assumed complete when the player's hands come to rest outside the pot area. (This rule is used because no-limit play may require a large number of chips be put into the pot.)

9. A bet of a single chip or bill without comment is considered to be the full amount of the chip or bill allowed. However, a player acting on a previous bet with a larger denomination chip or bill is calling the previous bet unless this player makes a verbal declaration to raise the pot. (This includes acting on the forced bet of the big blind.)

10. If a player tries to bet or raise less than the legal minimum and has more chips, the wager must be increased to the proper size. (This does not apply to a player who has unintentionally put too much in to call.) The wager is brought up to the sufficient amount only, no greater size.

11. All wagers may be required to be in the same denomination of chip (or larger) used for the minimum bring-in, even if smaller chips are used in the blind structure. If this is done, the smaller chips do not play except in quantity, even when going all-in.

12. In non-tournament games, one optional live straddle is allowed. The player who posts the straddle has last action for the first round of betting and is allowed to raise. To straddle, a player must be on the immediate left of the big blind, and must post an amount twice the size of the big blind.

13. In all no-limit and pot-limit games, the house has the right to place a maximum time limit for taking action on your hand. The clock may be put on someone by the dealer as directed by a floorperson, if a player requests it. If the clock is put on you when you are facing a bet, you will have one additional minute to act on your hand. You will have a ten-second warning, after which your hand is dead if you have not acted.

14. "Insurance" or any other "proposition wagers" are not allowed. Players are asked to refrain from instigating proposition wagers in any form. The players are allowed to agree to deal twice (or three times) when someone is all-in. "Dealing twice" means the pot is divided in two, with each portion being dealt for separately.

14.2: POT-LIMIT RULES

1. If a wager is made that exceeds the pot size, the surplus will be given back to the bettor as soon as possible, and the amount will be reduced to the maximum allowable.
2. The dealer or any player in the game can and should call attention to a wager that appears to exceed the pot size (this also applies to heads-up pots). The oversize wager may be corrected at any point until all players have acted on it.
3. If an oversize wager has stood for a length of time with someone considering what action to take, that person has had to act on a wager that was thought to be a certain size. If the player then decides to call or raise, and attention is called at this late point to whether this is an allowable amount, the floorperson may rule that the oversize amount must stand (especially if the person now trying to reduce the amount is the person that made the wager).
4. The maximum amount a player can raise is the amount in the pot after the call is made. Therefore, if a pot is $100, and someone makes a $50 bet, the next player can call $50 and raise the pot $200, for a total wager of $250.
5. In pot-limit play, it is advisable in many structures to round off the pot size upward to produce a faster pace of play. This is done by treating any odd amount as the next larger size. For example, if the pot size was being kept track of with $25 units, then a pot size of $80 would be treated as a pot size of $100.
6. In pot-limit hold 'em and pot-limit Omaha, many structures treat the little blind as if it were the same size of the big blind in computing pot size. In such a structure, a player can open for a maximum of four times the size of the big blind. For example, if the blinds are $5 and $10, a player may open with a raise to $40. (The range of options is to either open with a call of $10, or raise in increments of five dollars to any amount from $20 to $40.) Subsequent players also treat the $5 as if it were $10 in computing the pot size, until the big blind is through acting on the first betting round.
7. In pot-limit, if a chip or a bill larger than the pot size is put into the pot without comment, it is considered to be a bet of the pot size.

15.0: TOURNAMENTS

By participating in any tournament, you agree to abide by the rules and behave in a courteous manner. A violator may be verbally warned, suspended from play for a specified length of time, or disqualified from the tournament. Chips from a disqualified participant will be removed from play.

1. Whenever possible, all rules are the same as those that apply to live games.

2. Initial seating is determined by random draw or assignment. (For a one-table event, cards to determine seating may be left face-up so the earlier entrants can pick their seat, since the button is assigned randomly.)

3. The appropriate starting amount of chips will be placed on the table for each paid entrant at the beginning of the event, whether the person is present or not. Absent players will be dealt in, and all chips necessary for antes and blinds will be put into the pot.

4. If a paid entrant is absent at the start of an event, at some point an effort will be made to locate and contact the player. If the player requests the chips be left in place until arrival, the request will be honored. If the player is unable to be contacted, the chips may be removed from play at the discretion of the director anytime after a new betting level is begun or a half-hour has elapsed, whichever occurs first.

5. A starting stack of chips may be placed in a seat to accommodate late entrants (so all antes and blinds have been appropriately paid). An unsold seat will have such a stack removed at a time left to the discretion of the director.

6. Limits and blinds are raised at regularly scheduled intervals.

7. If there is a signal designating the end of a betting level, the new limits apply on the next deal. (A deal begins with the first riffle of the shuffle.)

8. The lowest denomination of chip in play will be removed from the table when it is no longer needed in the blind or ante structure. All lower-denomination chips that are of sufficient quantity for a new chip will be changed up directly. The method for removal of odd chips is to deal one card to a player for each odd chip possessed. Cards are dealt clockwise starting with the 1-seat, with each player receiving all cards before any cards are dealt to the

next player. The player with the highest card by suit gets enough odd chips to exchange for one new chip, the second-highest card gets to exchange for the next chip, and so forth, until all the lower-denomination chips are exchanged. A player may not be eliminated from the event by the chip-change process. If a player has no chips after the race has been held, that player will be given a chip of the higher denomination before anyone else is awarded a chip. If an odd number of lower-denomination chips are left after this process, the player with the highest card remaining will receive a new chip if having half or more of the quantity of lower-denomination chips needed, otherwise nothing.

9. An absent player is always dealt a hand, and will be put up for blinds, antes, and the forced bet if low.

10. A player must be present at the table to stop the action by calling "time."

11. A player must be at the table by the time all players have their complete starting hands in order to have a live hand for that deal. (The dealer has been instructed to kill the hands of all absent players immediately after dealing each player a starting hand.)

12. As players are eliminated, tables are broken in a pre-set order, with players from the broken tables assigned to empty seats at other tables.

13. A change of seat is not allowed after play starts, except as assigned by the director.

14. In button games, if a player is needed to move from a table to balance tables, the player due for the big blind will be automatically selected to move, and will be given the earliest seat due for the big blind if more than one seat is open.

15. New players are dealt in immediately and take over the obligations of that position, including the small blind or button position.

16. The number of players at each table will be kept reasonably balanced by the transfer of a player as needed. With more than six tables, table size will be kept within two players. With six tables or less, table size will be kept within one player.

17. In all contests using three or more tables, there is a redraw for seating when the field is reduced to two tables, and again to one table.

18. A player who declares all in and loses the pot, then discovers that one or more chips were hidden, is not entitled to benefit from this.

That player is eliminated from the tournament if the opponent had sufficient chips to cover the hidden ones (A rebuy is okay if allowable by the rules of that event). If another deal has not yet started, the director may rule the chips belong to the opponent who won that pot, if that obviously would have happened with the chips out in plain view. If the next deal has started, the discovered chips are removed from the tournament.

19. If a player lacks sufficient chips for a blind or a forced bet, the player is entitled to get action on whatever amount of money remains. A player who posts a short blind and wins does not need to make up the blind.

20. All players must leave their seat immediately after being eliminated from an event.

21. Showing cards from a live hand during the action injures the rights of other players still competing in an event, who wish to see contestants eliminated. A player may not show any cards during a deal (unless the event has only two remaining players). If a player deliberately shows a card, the player may be penalized (but his hand will not be ruled dead). Verbally stating one's hand during the play may be penalized.

22. The limit on raises is also applied to heads-up situations (except the last two players in a tournament are exempted from a limitation on raises).

23. At pot-limit and no-limit play, the player must either use a verbal statement giving the amount of the raise or put the chips into the pot in a single motion. Otherwise, it is a string bet.

24. Non-tournament chips are not allowed on the table.

25. Higher-denomination chips must be placed where they are easily visible to all other players at the table.

26. All tournament chips must remain visible on the table throughout the event. Chips taken off the table or pocketed will be removed from the event, and a player who is caught doing this may be disqualified.

27. Inappropriate behavior like throwing cards that go off the table may be punished with a penalty such as being dealt out for a length of time. A severe infraction such as abusive or disruptive behavior may be punished by eviction from the tournament.

28. The deck is not changed on request. Decks change when the dealers change, unless there is a damaged card.

29. In all tournament games using a dealer button, the starting position of the button is determined by the players drawing for the high card.

30. The dealer button remains in position until the appropriate blinds are taken. Players must post all blinds every round. Because of this, last action may be given to the same player for two consecutive hands by the use of a "dead button." [See 16.0: Explanations, discussion #1, for more information on this rule.]

31. In heads-up play with two blinds, the small blind is on the button.

32. At stud, if a downcard on the initial hand is dealt face-up, a misdeal is called.

33. If a player announces the intent to rebuy before cards are dealt, that player is playing behind and is obligated to make the rebuy.

34. All hands will be turned face-up whenever a player is all-in and betting action is complete.

35. If two (or more) players go broke during the same hand, the player starting the hand with the larger amount of money finishes in the higher tournament place for prize money and any other award.

36. Management is not required to rule on any private deals, side bets, or redistribution of the prize pool among finalists.

37. Private agreements by remaining players in an event regarding distribution of the prize pool are not condoned. (However, if such an agreement is made, the director has the option of ensuring that it is carried out by paying those amounts.) Any private agreement that excludes one or more active competitors is improper by definition.

38. A tournament event is expected to be played until completion. A private agreement that removes all prize money from being at stake in the competition is unethical.

39. Management retains the right to cancel any event, or alter it in a manner fair to the players.

16.0: EXPLANATIONS

1. The only place in this set of rules that an alternative is mentioned other than in this section is in the method of button and blind placement. That rule (the first rule in "Section 4 – Button and Blind Use") is repeated below for convenience.

   "Each round all participating players must get an opportunity for the button, and meet the total amount of the blind obligations. Either of the following methods of button and blind placement may be designated to do this:

   (a) Moving button – The button always moves forward to the next player and the blinds adjust accordingly. There may be more than one big blind.

   (b) Dead button – The big blind is posted by the player due for it, and the small blind and button are positioned accordingly, even if this means the small blind or the button is placed in front of an empty seat, giving the same player the privilege of last action on consecutive hands."

   Poker tradition has a lot to do with the fact that both of these methods are in widespread use, but neither method is superior in all situations. The moving button makes sure no player gets the advantage of last action twice on a round (a big advantage at no-limit or pot-limit play). On the other hand, a player may get to post a blind when on the button, which is more advantageous than posting in front of the button. The moving button creates a situation where two big blinds may be posted on a deal, which speeds up the action. At tournament play this speed-up can be undesirable, as when dealing is being done hand-for-hand to balance the pace of play between two remaining tables. A cardroom may either decide for the sake of simplicity to use only one method, or decide to tailor the method to the game and situation.

2. The rules given for rectifying a hold 'em situation where the dealer has dealt the flop or another boardcard before all the betting action on a round are inferior, because the dealer is told to not burn a card on a redeal. Since the "no burn" rule is so common, there was no choice but to use it here. But at some point it would be good for poker for some major cardrooms to get together and agree to use the better rule, or a gaming commission to require the better rule

be used. Here is the rules in question (the third rule and fourth rule in 5.0: Hold 'Em).

> "If the cards are prematurely flopped before the betting is complete, or if the flop contains too many cards, the boardcards are mixed with the remainder of the deck. The burncard remains on the table. After shuffling, the dealer cuts the deck and deals a new flop without burning a card."

> "If the dealer turns the fourth card on the board before the betting round is complete, the card is taken out of play for that round, even if subsequent players elect to fold. The betting is then completed. The dealer burns and turns what would have been the fifth card in the fourth card's place. After this round of betting, the dealer reshuffles the deck, including the card that was taken out of play, but not including the burncards or discards. The dealer then cuts the deck and turns the final card without burning a card. (If the fifth card is turned up prematurely, the deck is reshuffled and dealt in the same manner.)"

> The portion of this rule saying the dealer does not burn a card on the redeal is misguided. It is much harder for the dealer to control the card to be dealt if a burn is required. The applicable sentence in the rule should read, "The dealer then cuts the deck, burns a card, and turns the final card."

3. Rule seven in "Section 4 – Button and Blind Use" says, "A new player cannot be dealt in between the big blind and the button. Blinds may not be made up between the big blind and the button. You must wait until the button passes." This rule is standard practice, but allowing a new player or player making up blinds to come in between the blinds is better (if the dealer knows how to handle the resulting situations), because it gets players eager to join or rejoin the game into action faster.

4. Most poker rule sets say you have a dead hand at the showdown if you do not have the proper number of cards for that game. At stud, this rule is too strict. An inexperienced player sometimes does not pay sufficient attention to the final card when holding a big hand like a flush or full house (where improvement is neither likely to happen nor be needed), and fails to protect that card. If the dealer

erroneously puts that final card into the muck after the player fails to take it in, the rules should give the decision-maker an option to rule such a hand live. Rule 18 in 8.0: Seven-Card Stud reads as below:

"A hand with more than seven cards is dead. A hand with less than seven cards at the showdown is dead, except any player missing a seventh card may have the hand ruled live."

5. This rulebook requires all cash to be changed into chips. In some games this can be a bit impractical for various reasons. If the game chooses to allow cash, only large bills should be permitted.

6. Most poker rulebooks follow the usual California practice in multihanded pots at limit poker of allowing a bet and six raises for lowball and draw high. The number of allowable raises for those games is given in this rulebook as a bet and three raises because this cuts down on the effect of collusion between players, and more raises than three are seldom needed to define the strength of two hands when another player is calling.

7. Lowball has historically had less stringent demands on the order of cards or acceptability of exposed cards than in most other poker forms. This rulebook follows the modern trend at lowball regarding misdeals of requiring the cards to be dealt face-down and in proper order.

8. At ace-to-five limit lowball, an exposed card rule used less often, but probably a superior rule, is to not let a player take an exposed six or seven (the rule for no-limit ace-to-five lowball). If a player gets to keep only a card that might make a perfect hand, having a card exposed is less advantageous, and the opponent must reckon with the possibility of a perfect hand.

9. At lowball and draw high, some rule sets allow a player to draw five consecutive cards. The rule used here disallowing this makes cheating more difficult. Our rule #10 in lowball and rule #5 in draw high says, "A player may draw up to four consecutive cards. If a player wishes to draw five new cards, four are dealt right away, and the fifth card after everyone else has drawn cards. If the last player wishes to draw five new cards, four are dealt right away, and a card is burned before the player receives a fifth card."

10. In tournament play, there are two ways the hand of an absent player may be treated. Our rule #11 in 15.0: Tournaments, is: "If you are not present when it becomes your turn to act, your

hand is dead. This includes situations in which a live blind is not present to act, since an absent player cannot exercise the option to raise." This speeds up play, and also prevents a player from facing situations like thinking he is moving all-in heads-up against a short stack and an absent player comes back to the table to enter the pot. The alternative is: "If a player is absent, the hand shall not be killed until that seat faces a wager. An absent player's hand is dead at the showdown." This rule gives the absent player the maximum amount of time to return and be able to play the hand.

POKER TOURNAMENT DIRECTORS ASSOCIATION RULES

Reprinted courtesy of the Poker Tournament Directors Association

The Poker Tournament Directors Association (TDA), founded in 2001, is a non-profit organization originally comprised of tournament directors and poker room managers who collaborated to draft a standardized set of poker rules specifically applied to poker tournaments. Members of the association meet periodically to discuss, add to, or amend the tournament rules.

Matt Savage sparked the idea for developing the organization after playing in several tournaments where the rules were inconsistent and the rulings often incorrect. He proposed the idea in 2001 to Bob Thompson, the World Series of Poker Tournament Director, but was told that it had been tried many times to no avail. Matt then pitched the idea to his friend Linda Johnson, a major influence in the poker world. Linda invited David Lamb and Jan Fisher into the discussion and provided a venue to hold the first meeting of the TDA a month later. The organization, which started with 25 tournament directors, now includes nearly 400 members from around the world.

Tournament driectors all over the world run tournaments using the TDA rules, although there are sometimes modifications to tehse rules to allow for local gaming regulations and customs. Membership to the organization is free and all poker players, tournament directors and media representatives are encouraged to participate. Additional information about the Poker Tournament Directors Association can be found at www.pokertda.com.

Floor People

Floor people are to consider the best interest of the game and fairness as the top priority in the decision-making process. Unusual circumstances can, on occasion, dictate that the technical interpretation of the rules be ignored in the interest of fairness. The floor person's decision is final.

Chip Race

When it is time to color-up chips, they will be raced off with a maximum of one chip going to any player. The chip race will always start in the No. 1 seat. A player cannot be raced out of a tournament. A player who loses his or her remaining chip(s) in a chip race will be given one chip of the smallest denomination still in play. Players are encouraged to witness the chip race.

Odd Chips

The odd chip(s) will go to the high hand. In flop games, when there are two or more high hands or two or more low hands, the odd chip(s) will go to the left of the button. In stud games, the odd chip will go to the high card by suit. However, when hands have identical value (i.e., a wheel in Omaha/8) the pot will be split as evenly as possible.

Side Pots

Each side pot will be split separately.

Calling for a Clock

Once a reasonable amount of time has passed and a clock is called for, a player will be given a maximum of one minute to make a decision. If action has not been taken before time expires, there will be a 10-second countdown. If a player has not acted by the time the countdown is over, the player's hand will be dead.

Dead Button

Tournament play will use a dead button.

Penalties and Disqualification

A penalty *may* be invoked if a player exposes any card with action pending, throws a card off the table, violates the one-player-to-a-hand rule, or similar incidents take place. Penalties *will* be invoked in cases of soft play, abuse, or disruptive behavior. Penalties available to the

Tournament Director include verbal warnings and "missed hand" penalties. A missed hand penalty will be assessed as follows: The offender will miss one hand for every player, including the offender, who is at the table when the penalty is given multiplied by the number of rounds specified in the penalty. For the period of the penalty the offender should remain away from the table. Tournament staff can assess one, two, three, or four-round penalties or disqualification. A player who is disqualified shall have his or her chips removed from play. Repeat infractions are subject to escalating penalties.

At Your Seat

A player must be at his or her seat by the time all players have been dealt complete initial hands in order to have a live hand. Players must be at their seat to call time.

Face Up

All cards will be turned face up once a player is all-in and all betting action is complete.

Raise Requirements

If a player puts in a raise of 50% or more of the previous bet but less than the minimum raise, he or she will be required to make a full raise. The raise will be exactly the minimum raise allowed. In no-limit and pot-limit, an all-in bet of less than a full raise does not reopen the betting to a player who has already acted.

Oversized Chip

A single oversized chip will be considered a call if the player does not announce a raise. If a player puts an oversized chip into the pot and states raise but does not state the amount, the raise will be the maximum allowable up to the size of that chip. After the flop, an initial bet of a single oversized chip without comment will constitute the size of the bet. To make a raise with a single oversized chip, a verbal declaration must be made before the chip hits the table surface.

No Disclosure, No Advice, One Player to a Hand

Players are obligated to protect the other players in the tournament at all times. Therefore, players, whether in the hand or not, may not:
1. Disclose the contents of live or folded hands
2. Advise or criticize play before the action is complete
3. Read a hand that has not been tabled

The one-player-to-a-hand rule will be enforced.

Random Seats

Tournament and satellite seats will be randomly assigned.

Official Language

The English-only rule will be enforced in the United States during the play of hands. English will be used in international play along with the local or native language.

Communication Devices

A player may not use a cellular phone, text-messaging device or other communication device at the table.

Foreign Chips

There will be no foreign chips on the table except for a maximum of one card cap.

Deck Changes

Deck changes will be on the dealer push or level changes or as prescribed by the house. Players may not ask for deck changes.

New Limits

When time has elapsed in a round and a new level is announced by a member of the tournament staff, the new level applies to the next hand. A hand begins with the first riffle.

Re-buys

A player may not miss a hand. If a player announces the intent to re-buy before a new hand begins, that player is playing chips behind and is obligated to make the re-buy.

Higher Denomination Chips Visible

Players must keep their higher denomination chips visible at all times.

Declarations

Verbal declarations as to the content of a player's hand are not binding; however, any player deliberately miscalling his or her hand may be penalized.

Rabbit Hunting

No rabbit hunting is allowed.

Dodging Blinds

A player who intentionally dodges a blind(s) when moving from a broken table will incur a penalty.

Chips Visible

All chips must be visible at all times. Players may not hold or transport tournament chips in any manner that takes them out of view. A player who does so will forfeit the chips and will face disqualification. The forfeited chips will be taken out of play.

Breaking Tables

Players going from a broken table to fill in seats assume the rights and responsibilities of the position. They can get the big blind, the small blind or the button. The only place they cannot get a hand is between the small blind and the button.

Balancing Tables

In flop games when balancing tables, players will be moved from the big blind to the worst position (which is never the small blind). The table to which a player is moved will be as specified by a predetermined procedure. Play will halt on any table that is at least three players short. In stud games, players will be moved by position (the last seat to open up at the short table is the seat to be filled).

Raises

There is no cap on the number of raises in no-limit games. A raise must be at least the size of the previous raise. In limit events, there will be a limit to raises, even when heads-up, until the tournament is down to two players; the house limit will apply.

Misdeals

In stud games, if any of the players' two down cards are exposed due to dealer error, it is a misdeal. In flop games, exposure of one of the first two cards dealt is a misdeal. Players may be dealt two consecutive cards on the button.

Unprotected Hands

If a dealer kills an unprotected hand, the player will have no redress and will not be entitled to a refund of bets. However, if a player had raised and the raise had not yet been called, the raise will be returned to the player.

Killing Winning Hand

Dealers cannot kill a winning hand that was tabled and was obviously the winning hand. Players are encouraged to assist in reading tabled hands if it appears that an error is about to be made.

Verbal Declarations

Verbal declarations in turn are binding. Action out of turn may be binding and will be binding if the action to that player has not changed. A check, call or fold is not considered action-changing.

Exposing Cards

A player who exposes his or her cards with action pending may incur a penalty, but will not have a dead hand. The penalty will begin at the end of the hand.

Methods of Raising

In no-limit or pot-limit, a raise must be made by (1) placing the full amount in the pot in one motion; or (2) verbally declaring the full amount prior to the initial placement of chips into the pot; or (3) verbally declaring "raise" prior to the placement of the amount to call into the pot and then completing the action with one additional motion.

Ethical Play

Poker is an individual game. Soft play will result in penalties which may include forfeiture of chips and/or disqualification. Chip dumping will result in disqualification.

Pot Size

Players are entitled to be informed of the pot size in pot-limit games only. Dealers will not count the pot in limit and no-limit games.

Button in Heads-up

When heads-up, the small blind is on the button and acts first. When beginning heads-up play, the button may need to be adjusted to ensure that no player takes the big blind twice in a row.

Etiquette Violations

Repeated etiquette violations will result in penalties. Examples include unnecessarily touching other players cards or chips, delay of the game, and excessive chatter. Players are required to act in turn.

Showdown

At the end of the last round of betting, the player who made the last aggressive action in that betting round must show first. If there was no bet, the player to the left of the button shows first and so on clockwise.

In stud games, the player with the high board must show first. In Razz, the lowest board shows first.

Action Pending

Players must remain at the table if they still have action pending on a hand.

String Raises

Dealers will be responsible for calling string raises.

Playing the Board

A player must show both cards when playing the board in order to get part of the pot.

WORLD SERIES OF POKER RULES

Reprinted by permission of the World Series of Poker®
Word Series of Poker is a registered trademark of Harrahs License Company LLC

The World Series of Poker (WSOP) is a series of poker tournaments held annually at Harrah's Rio Casino in Las Vegas, Nevada. The series started with a single invitational event at Jack Binion's Horseshoe Casino in 1970 where Johnny Moss was declared the World Champion by popular vote of fellow players. The following year, players competed in a single freeze-out game where the champion was designated as the last player with chips at the table. Johnny Moss, once again, was declared the World Champion. Every year since, the competition has been tournament style, increasing from a single event of seven players to over 30 tournaments of various types of poker, with the 2006 main event hosting 8,773 players.

The growing number of participants at the World Series of Poker has had a profound affect on the establishment and enforcement of game rules. *Robert's Rules of Poker* and the Poker Tournament Directors Association rules are the foundation for rules enforced during all WSOP events. Harrah's compiled information from both sources to write ninety-three rules related specifically to the World Series of Poker. These rules are followed at the WSOP and all WSOP Circuit Events, which take place throughout the year at various casinos. The rules for the WSOP Circuit Events are sometimes altered to meet local regulations.

Out of the 93 WSOP rules, specific poker game rules are included in this section. All other rules, related to WSOP registration and eligibility, have been omitted. Additional information about the World Series of Poker can be found at www.worldseriesofpoker.com.

41. Chip race rule: Race-off is defined as removal of a denomination chip no longer in use. When it is time to color-up chips, they will be raced off with a maximum of one chip going to any player. The chip race will always start at the first player left of the dealer. A player cannot be raced out of a tournament. In the event that a

player has only one chip remaining, the regular race procedure will take place. If that player loses the race, [s]he will be given one chip of the smallest denomination still in play.

42. Side pots: Each side pot will be split as a separate pot. Pots will not be mixed together before they are split. The odd chip(s) will go to the high hand. In flop games, when there are two (2) or more high hands or two (2) or more low hands, the odd chip(s) will go to the left of the button. In stud-type games, the odd chip will go to the high card by suit. However, when hands have identical value, e.g., a wheel in Omaha 8 or Better, the pot will be split as evenly as possible.

43. Calling-for-clock procedures: Once a reasonable amount of time has passed and a clock is called, a player will be given one (1) minute to act. If action has not been taken by the time the minute has expired, there will be a ten (10) second countdown. If a player has not acted on his hand by the time the countdown is over, the hand will be dead.

44. Dead Button: Tournament play will use the dead button rule. Dead Button is defined as a button that can not be advanced due to elimination of a player or the seating of a new player into a position between the small blind and the button.

45. A player exposing his or her cards with action pending may incur a penalty, but will not have a dead hand. The penalty will begin at the end of the hand. A penalty may also be imposed if a player throws a card off the table, violates the one-player-to-a-hand rule or engages in similar behavior. Penalties will be invoked in cases of soft-play, abuse or disruptive behavior. All penalties will be imposed at Harrah's sole and absolute discretion, in accordance with Rule No. 46.

46. In its sole and absolute discretion, Harrah's may impose penalties that include verbal warnings and missed-hand penalties. A missed-hand penalty will be assessed as follows: The offender will miss one hand for each player at the table, including the offender, when the penalty is given, multiplied by the number of rounds specified in the penalty. Tournament staff can assess one-, two-, three- or four-round penalties or disqualification. Repeat infractions are subject to escalating penalties. A player who is disqualified shall have his or her chips removed from play and no refund will be provided to that disqualified player.

47. A player must be at his or her seat by the time all players have been dealt complete initial hands to have a live hand. Players must be at their seats to call time.

48. All cards will be turned face up once a player is all in and all action is complete.

49. If a player puts in a raise of 50 percent or more of the previous bet but less than the minimum raise, he or she will be required to make a full raise. The raise will be exactly the minimum raise allowed. In no-limit and pot-limit, an all-in bet of less than a full raise does not reopen the betting to a player who has already acted. Putting a single oversized chip into the pot will be considered a call if the player doesn't announce a raise. If a player puts an oversized chip into the pot and says, "Raise," but doesn't state the amount, the raise will be the maximum allowable up to the denomination of that chip. To make a raise with a single oversized chip, a verbal declaration must be made before the chip hits the table surface. After the flop, an initial bet of a single oversized chip without comment will constitute the size of the bet.

50. In no-limit or pot-limit, a raise must be made by a.) placing the full amount in the pot in one motion or b.) verbally declaring the full amount prior to the initial placement of chips into the pot or c.) verbally declaring "raise" prior to the placement of the amount to call into the pot and then completing the action with one additional motion. Less than a full raise in an all-in situation does not reopen the betting to a player who has already acted.

51. Players are obligated to protect the other players in the tournament at all times. Therefore, whether in a hand or not, players may not a.) disclose contents of live or folded hands, b.) advise or criticize play before the action is completed or c.) read a hand that hasn't been tabled. The one-player-to-a-hand rule will be enforced. Players who violate this rule are subject to penalty in accordance with Rule 46.

52. Tournament and satellite seats will be randomly assigned.

53. The English-only rule will be enforced at the WSOP during the play of hands.

54. There will be no foreign objects on the table except for a maximum of one card cap. Card caps can be no larger than two (2) inches in diameter and no more than one-half (1/2) inch in depth.

55. Deck changes will be on the dealer push or limit changes or as prescribed by Harrah's. Players may not ask for deck changes unless a card is damaged.

56. When time has elapsed in a round and a new round is announced, the new limits apply to the next hand. A hand begins with the first riffle.

57. If a player announces the intent to re-buy before the first card is dealt, that player is playing behind and is obligated to make the re-buy. If a player runs out of chips during the re-buy portion of a re-buy event, he must be-buy or declare to re-buy before the start of the next deal.

58. Players must keep their highest denomination chips visible at all times.

59. Verbal declarations as to the content of a player's hand are not binding; however at Harrah's discretion, any player deliberately miscalling his hand may be penalized.

60. In cases where hands are concluded prior to the last card being dealt, the next card to be dealt will not be exposed under any circumstances. This prohibited practice is commonly referred to as "rabbit hunting."

61. A player who intentionally dodges his or her blind(s) when moving from a broken table will incur a penalty, in accordance with Rule No. 46.

62. All chips must be visible at all times. Players may not hold or transport tournament chips in any manner that takes them out of view. A player who does so will forfeit the chips and face disqualification. The forfeited chips will be taken out of play.

63. The breaking order for an event will be posted at the beginning of that event. The table to which a player is moved will be specified by a predetermined procedure. Play will halt at any table that is at least three players short. Players going from a broken table to fill in seats assume the rights and responsibilities of the position. They can get the big blind, the small blind or the button. The only place they cannot get a hand is between the small blind and the button. In flop games, players will be moved from the big blind to the worst position (which is never the small blind) at the new table. In stud games, players will be moved by position (the last seat to open up at the short table is the seat to be filled). Harrah's reserves the right to alter the breaking order due to unusual circumstances.

64. There is no cap on the number of raises in no-limit games. A raise must be at least the size of the previous raise. In limit events, there will be a limit of one bet and four raises even when heads up until the tournament is down to two players. Once the tournament becomes heads-up, the rule does not apply. There may be unlimited raises at the heads-up level.

65. In stud-type games, if any of the players' two down cards are exposed due to a dealer error, it is a misdeal. In flop games, exposure of one of the first two cards dealt is a misdeal. Players may be dealt two consecutive cards on the button.

66. If a dealer kills an unprotected hand, the player will have no redress and will not be entitled to his or her money back. An exception would be if a player raised and his or her raise had not been called yet, he or she would be entitled to receive his or her raise back.

67. A dealer cannot kill a winning hand that was turned face up and was obviously the winning hand. Players are encouraged to assist in reading tabled hands if it appears that an error is about to be made.

68. Harrah's reserves the right to cancel or alter any event at its sole discretion in the best interest of the casino or its players.

69. Poker is an individual game. Soft play will result in penalties that may include forfeiture of chips and/or disqualification. Chip dumping will result in disqualification.

70. Players are entitled to be informed of the pot size in pot-limit games only. Dealers will not count the pot in limit and no-limit games.

71. When heads up in blind games, the small blind is on the button and acts first. When beginning heads-up play, the button may need to be adjusted to ensure no player takes the big blind twice.

72. At the end of the last round of betting, the player who made the last aggressive betting action in that betting round must show first. If there was no bet, the player to the left of the button shows first, and so on in a clockwise direction. In stud games, the player with the high board must show first. In Razz, the lowest board shows first.

73. Players must remain at the table if they still have action pending on a hand.

74. Dealers will be responsible for calling string raises.

75. A player must show cards when playing the board to get part of the pot.

76. Any player registering for multiple events and who makes Day Two or the final table of a particular event, may transfer his or her buy-in for the subsequent event to another event, or may also receive a refund, upon request, provided that the transfer or refund is approved and initiated prior to the beginning of the event from which a transfer or refund is being requested.

77. Players are responsible for checking their tournament entry receipts before they leave the registration window. All changes must be made before the start of any event.

78. If an event is sold to capacity when that event begins, all alternates will receive a full chip stack when their seat becomes available.

79. Registration is open until the end of the first level of any event.

80. Late registrants for any event may incur a chip penalty. Players will lose one round of blinds/antes dead money into the pot for every 15 minutes late after a tournament has begun up to a maximum of three (3) rounds of blinds/antes.

81. Cell Phone Rule: A player who wants to use a cellular phone must step away from the table. Any player on the cell phone or texting a messaging when the dealer delivers the first card from the deck will have a dead hand. No cell phones can be placed on a poker table.

82. Approved Electronic Device Rule: Players are allowed to use as approved electronic devices iPods, MP3 and other music players or noise-reduction headsets during tournament play until they have reached the money, so long as the approved electronic devices are not equipped with any type of communication device. Once players are in the money for any tournament, all approved electronic devices must be removed. An announcement will be made to players once they have reached the money to remove all such electronic devices. Failure to do so will result in a penalty up to and including disqualification.

83. At the end of a hand, if a player exposes one hole card, he or she must also show the other hole card if asked to do so by any player.

84. All chips put into the pot in turn stay in the pot. If a player has raised and his or her hand is killed before the raise is called, the player may be entitled to the raise back, but will forfeit the amount of the call. Any chips put into the pot out of turn fall under action "may or may not be binding".

85. Players must act in turn at all times. Action out of turn may or may not be binding. If a player acts out of turn and the action does not change by the time it is that player's turn to act, that player's action is binding. Action only changes by a player raising before the action gets back to the person that acted out of turn. Action does not change when the player in front of a player acting out of turn calls or folds. If a player acts out of turn and the action changes, the person who acted out of turn may change their action by calling, raising or folding and may have their chips returned. Players will receive a warning for the first occurrence of acting out of turn, and will receive a penalty, in accordance with Rule No. 46, every time after.

CHAPTER THREE

POKER ETIQUETTE

Formal rules of poker dictate how a poker game is to be played, whereas poker etiquette determines how smoothly a poker game will flow. Cardroom management and players may sometimes overlook poor behavior, or simply issue a warning to unruly players. Breaking certain rules of etiquette can result in suspension or dismissal from a cardroom.

A player adhering to proper poker etiquette will earn respect from other players and contribute to the enjoyment of the game. The following guidelines outline the proper code of conduct expected from players in a standard poker game:

Basic Knowledge

Players entering a new game should have a basic understanding of poker, including hand rankings, calling, betting and folding procedures.

Be Tolerant of New Players

Seasoned players should keep in mind that every new player makes mistakes. Players should be patient as new players familiarize themselves with dealing patterns, blind structures and betting routines. Instead of berating a player for ignorance, it is more sensible to help that player gain knowledge about the process and feel comfortable enough to return to the game.

Acting out of Turn

A player should always follow the action around the table and fold, call or raise only when the action is to that player. Acting out of turn gives an unfair advantage to other players at the table.

Slowing Down the Game

Players should act within a reasonable amount of time in order to keep up the pace of the game. When other players repeatedly call the clock on a specific player, it can be assumed the player is purposely slowing down the game. Every hand should not require a lengthy time for decision making.

Splashing the Pot

Throwing chips into the pot, also known as "splashing the pot," is considered poor poker etiquette. It makes it difficult for the players as well as the dealer to determine the amount entered into the pot, or the accurate amount placed when a player is calling a bet. The preferred method would be to stack the chips in easy-to-count increments or slide them forward and allow the dealer to count the chips. Verbally declaring the betting amount is also helpful and reduces confusion over the actual chip count.

Cell Phones

Talking on a cellular phone during a poker game is improper and can be distracting to other players. It is courteous to switch cell phones from ring mode to vibrate or silent mode and leave the table when talking on the phone.

Headphones and MP3 Players

Players should always keep the volume on their headphones or MP3 players low enough that other poker players are not forced to listen to distracting music. A player using such a device should pause or lower the volume on the device during a hand in order to hear any comments or questions from the dealer.

Swearing

In most poker settings, swearing is not an infraction of the rules; however, it is considered poor form under any circumstances.

Abusing the Dealer

Yelling at the dealer for mistakes or blaming the dealer for bad luck is unacceptable. If the dealer makes numerous mistakes, it is proper to contact the floorperson or houseperson to explain the situation and ask for a resolution or a dealer change.

The Dealer

It is the dealer's responsibility to keep the game flowing smoothly and remain focused at all times. It is unethical for a dealer to comment on player's hands, give players advice or peek at discarded cards. The dealer should not engage in idle chatter that may slow down the pace of the game.

Commenting During a Hand

It is improper to make comments about players involved in a hand or make predictions about the cards a player is holding during a hand. It is also inappropriate to make comments related to possible hands based on exposed cards, such as saying, "The flush got there" when a third spade is dealt in a community card game. Poker is not a team sport. Individual players should make their own analysis of the situation.

Avoiding the Blinds

In poker games where there are forced blind bets, it is considered poor etiquette to get up and leave the table numerous times in order to avoid posting a blind or playing hands from an unfavorable position.

Reacting to Community Cards

A player should never react to community cards when that player has already discarded the hand. For example, an inactive player who throws up his or her hand and grunts loudly when the board cards read K-5-5 is indicating that he or she discarded a five.

Hit and Run

Many players become agitated if an opponent enters a game for a short period of time, wins a big pot and immediately cashes in his or her chips. This is discouraging to players who want a chance to win their money back. However, a player should never be chastised for leaving a game. It is the right of every player to enter and exit the game at any time.

Getting Back into the Game

It is considered poor form to book a big win, leave the game briefly and then return and buy in for less than the amount previously won. Many casinos will allow players to do this, in fact, most large cardrooms have no way of tracking this; however, players who feel they have been violated in this way, will remember the player's poor etiquette.

Touching Another Player's Chips

It is never proper to touch another player's chips. A player should always ask the opponent or the dealer for a chip count when the amount is in question.

Mis-Declaring a Hand

Even in games where the "cards speak" rule applies, a player should announce his hand accurately at the time of showdown. By stating his or her hand is a flush when in fact the player has a four-flush slows down the game. This is rude to players remaining in the hand as well as to the dealer who is responsible for announcing the winning hand.

Rabbit Hunting

Asking to see cards that would have appeared if a hand continued play, also known as "rabbit hunting," slows down the game. It is also insulting for a player who shows a successful bluff to ask the dealer, "Rabbit hunt to see if I would have won anyway."

Slow Rolling

At the point of showdown, a player convinced that he has the winning hand should promptly turn the cards face-up. Hesitating in order to briefly convince the other player that he or she has won is considered poor form.

Coffee Housing

Speaking during a hand in order to extract information from another player, also known as "coffee housing," is within the rules of play in many games; however, excessive questioning and hounding of another player causes unnecessary delay and may be irritating to other players.

Chopping the Blinds

In a cash game that uses blinds, when players at the table fold around to the small and big blind, it is appropriate for the remaining players to offer one another their blind bet back, also known as "chopping the blinds." One or both of the players may also refuse to chop and should not be chastised for exercising that right.

Asking to See Cards

A player should not tell another player to turn a hand face-up at the point of showdown. The dealer is responsible for asking a player to show a hand when necessary.

Mucked Cards

When a player mucks a losing hand that was called by another player, rules dictate that other players at the table may ask to see the mucked hand if it is easily identified; however, it is considered poor etiquette to ask to see a discarded hand except in a situation where collusion is suspected.

Speak Up

A player should alert the dealer if he recognizes a mistake, such as a mis-declared hand or an incorrect chip count that costs another player at the table. The dealer is then responsible for correcting the error.

Excessive Drinking

Drinking at the table is acceptable unless it creates obnoxious behavior that makes it difficult for other players to ignore or causes the offender's reflexes to slow down the game.

Chip Placement

Players should place chips within the dealers reach or across the betting line printed on some poker tables. The dealer should not have to stand from the dealer seat to pull chips into the pot or to push the chips to another player.

Discarding a Hand

Players should discard all cards within reach of the dealer and low enough that other players are not able to view the cards as they are being discarded.

Revealing a Hand

It is not proper for a player to reveal cards during a hand in play. This can affect other players in the hand and cause an uninvolved player to comment or react unnecessarily.

Soft Play

Players should exert the same level of competitiveness against all players at the table. It is inappropriate to check to a friend or family member in a situation that would merit a bet when a different player is the opponent.

Show one Show all

If a player reveals his or her cards to another player at the table, the cards should be shown to all players at the table so that the information does not give an unfair advantage to one player.

Stacking Chips

Creatively stacking chips into the form of tall towers at the table can hinder the view of the dealer, the cards and other players in addition to the fact that it disturbs the game when chips topple. Players should keep chips at a moderate height with the highest denomination chips in the front so that other players are aware of the amount of money at risk.

Destroying Cards

Throwing, tearing, crumpling or bending cards out of anger results in disruption to the game and undo costs to the house for card replacement.

Be Neat

It is courteous to keep each area of play clean of food, drinks and trash. Players snacking at the table should always be sure to wipe their hands so that food is not transferred to the cards and keep drinks in a proper drink holder to reduce the risk of spills.

Space

Players should be aware of the limited space at a full poker table and make every attempt to stay confined to the area around their seat.

Smoking

In cardrooms that allow smoking, players should always be aware of where their lighted cigarette is and courteous enough to blow smoke away from other players at the table. A player seated at a smoking table should not ask another player not to smoke; however, it is appropriate to ask for a seat change if necessary. Players should understand that cigars, pipe smoke and clove cigarettes are especially bothersome to most people. Complaints regarding smoke in a poker game should always be directed toward the houseperson who is responsible for declaring a game smoking or smoke-free.

Cashing In

After beating a player, it is courteous to allow that player to leave the table and/or cardroom before racing to cash in the winning chips.

Giving Lessons at the Table

It is considered poor poker etiquette to give another player lessons on how to play the game or specific hands while at the table.

Language

It is courteous to speak the proper language at the table. If the game consists of predominately English-speaking players, it is unethical to speak in a foreign language unfamiliar to other players at the table.

Lose with Grace

A player should always try to maintain his or her composure after losing a hand. It is courteous to tap the table and say, "good hand," or simply remain silent after losing to an opponent. It is never appropriate to yell at or berate other players based on the loss of a poker hand.

Win with Grace

A player should always try to maintain his or her composure after winning a hand. It is courteous to remain silent while raking in chips after beating an opponent. It is never appropriate to cheer loudly, dance around the table or ridicule the losing player.

Pay Attention

It is important to be aware of where the action is in a poker game. It is disruptive to other players when the dealer has to continuously remind a player that the action is on him or her.

Distractions

Televisions and stereos should be set at a moderately low volume so that players will not be distracted by the noise. Singing to music or cheering while watching a ball game may also distract other players who are trying to focus on the poker game.

Checking it Down

Two players should never make an agreement to check a hand down when a third player is all-in.

Tip the Dealer

It is standard courtesy after winning a pot to give the dealer a token of appreciation, usually a small percentage of the money in the pot.

Peeking

A player should not try to peek at another player's downcards; however, if an opponent carelessly reveals his cards, a player may exercise his right to look and should not be penalized for doing so.

Taking a Break

When a player leaves the table for a period longer than ten minutes, the dealer and floorperson should be notified. Most cardrooms will allow up to two players to take an extended break without being removed from the game. In cardrooms where it is permitted, offering to allow a waiting player to "play over" an absent player is a courteous gesture.

The House

The house dealer should inform the cardroom manager or houseperson when a player violates poker etiquette to a point that it creates an uncomfortable atmosphere or distraction for the other competitors. Cardroom management or the houseperson has an obligation to take action against the player repeatedly exhibiting poor poker etiquette.

The Books

The houseperson, as well as cardroom employees, should never openly discuss money that players have borrowed against the house. Unsettled debts should be resolved privately between the parties involved.

Say Thank You

When leaving a poker game it is courteous to thank the host as well as the dealer. Likewise, when hosting a poker game it is courteous to thank each player for coming to the poker game.

Online Poker Etiquette

Most etiquette rules applied to cardroom poker also apply to online poker play. There are a few extra tips that are specific to playing online poker.

Free Play

When learning to play poker or adjusting to online poker play, it is courteous to practice in the free games provided by most poker websites. This feature familiarizes players with the process of online play and reduces the risk of mistakes that may cost other players time and money.

Screen Names

When selecting a screen name, it is impolite to use derogatory words or descriptions that may be offensive to others.

Chat Feature

Just like excessive talking at a real table, players overusing the chat feature can be distracting to other players online. A player should never use the chat box to berate, needle or give lessons to other players in the game. Profanity is unacceptable and typing in all capital letters may be interpreted as screaming.

Advertising

It is inappropriate to use the chat box to advertise other poker websites or for business promotion of any kind.

Sitting Out

Players should not abuse the Sit Out feature provided by online poker sites. A player wishing to take an extended break or multiple breaks in a cash game should leave the game and open the seat to another player.

Sitting Out in a Tournament

The Sit Out feature is helpful during tournaments for players who do not wish to play a hand for an extended period of time. Most websites skip players using the Sit Out feature instead of using a time bank that halts the action in the tournament.

Pre-Select Boxes

Using the auto-post and pre-select boxes whenever possible helps keeps up the pace of the game.

Playing Slow

When playing multiple games simultaneously, a player should be aware of whether or not he or she is slowing down the pace of each game. A player should never play more games than he or she can keep up with.

Contacting Customer Service

A player suspecting foul play or collusion should contact the online customer support. Players should not overuse the customer support service and realize that it takes a few minutes in most cases to receive a response from support. It is not necessary to report the same problem more than one time.

CHAPTER FOUR

VARIANT POKER GAMES

Most variant poker games are derived from one of three popular types of poker: Community Card Poker, Draw Poker and Stud Poker. The directions for variant games that do not fall into one of these three categories are listed under Miscellaneous Poker Games. All of the games listed in this chapter have one thing in common – they follow the standard format for ranking poker hands.

There are hundreds of variations of poker played today. Some are games played in major tournaments such as the World Series of Poker and the World Poker Tour while many are games played in a home setting or dealer's choice game. An asterisk (*) in front of the game title denotes that it is a game currently played at the World Series of Poker.

The information included in this chapter provides typical directions for the flow of popular poker games. It should be noted that house rules may dictate changes in the game such as changes to the blind, ante and bring-in bets, wild card variations and betting intervals. Once the basics of each game are understood, refer to the end of the chapter for ideas on creating new variant poker games.

Community Card Poker Games

Community card poker is any poker game where the players share cards with other players to make their best poker hand. This type of poker has exploded in popularity in recent years due to televised events. Texas Hold 'Em and Omaha can be found in most casinos as well as in home games. Texas Hold 'Em is the game played every year at the main event of the World Series of Poker to determine the world champion poker player. Other community card games such as Bingo and Iron Cross are popular home game favorites.

Some games using community cards are played using antes and some are played using blinds. Typically, if playing a dealer's choice type game where play switches between several poker variants, antes are used. If the game stays the same for the duration of play, as in most casino games, typically blinds are used. Step one of "Game Play" for each variant community card game lists whether it is common to start the game using antes or blinds.

*Texas Hold 'Em

Other Names: Hold 'Em, Two-Card Hold 'Em

Type: Community Card

Number of Players: 2 to 11; usually limited to 10 players in casinos and tournaments.

Winning Hand: Highest rank. Hand consists of best five cards from a combination of two downcards and five community cards.

Game Play:
1) Post blinds.
2) Deal two cards face-down to each player. Follow with betting round.
3) Burn a card. Deal three community cards face-up in the middle of the table. Follow with betting round.
4) Burn a card. Deal a fourth community card face-up. Follow with betting round.
5) Burn a card. Deal a fifth community card face-up. Follow with betting round.
6) Showdown.

*Omaha

Other Names: Omaha Hold 'Em

Type: Community Card

Number of Players: 2 to 11; typically limited to 10 players in casinos and tournaments.

Winning Hand: Highest rank. Hand consists of best five cards from a combination of two out of four downcards and three out of five community cards.

Game Play:
  1) Post blinds.
  2) Deal four cards face-down to each player. Follow with betting round.
  3) Burn a card. Deal three community cards face-up in the middle of the table. Follow with betting round.
  4) Burn a card. Deal a fourth community card face-up. Follow with betting round.
  5) Burn a card. Deal a fifth community card face-up. Follow with betting round.
  6) Showdown.

*Omaha High-Low Split Eight or Better

Other Names: Omaha/8, Omaha High-Low, Omaha High-Low/8, Omaha Hi-Lo, Omaha 8 or Better

Type: Community Card

Number of Players: 2 to 11; typically limited to 10 players in casinos and tournaments.

Winning Hand: Highest rank and lowest rank split the pot. Hand consists of best (highest and/or lowest) five cards from a combination of two out of four downcards and three out of five community cards.

Game Play:
  Played the same as Omaha except the best high hand and the best low hand split the pot.

Note: 1: A low hand must be ranked eight-high or lower with no pairs to qualify for half the pot. Ace plays high and low. Straights and flushes do not count against a low hand. **2:** It is possible for one player to hold the best high hand as well as the best low hand and scoop the entire pot.

Pineapple

Type: Community Card

Number of Players: 2 to 11; usually limited to 10 players in casinos.

Winning Hand: Highest rank. Hand consists of best five cards from a combination of two out of three downcards and five community cards.

Game Play:
1) Post blinds.
2) Deal three cards face-down to each player. Follow with betting round.
3) Each player discards one downcard.
4) Burn a card. Deal three community cards face-up in the middle of the table. Follow with betting round.
5) Burn a card. Deal a fourth community card face-up. Follow with betting round.
6) Burn a card. Deal a fifth community card face-up. Follow with betting round.
7) Showdown.

Crazy Pineapple

Type: Community Card

Number of Players: 2 to 11; usually limited to 10 players in casinos.

Winning Hand: Highest rank. Hand consists of best five cards from a combination of two out of three downcards and five community cards.

Game Play:
1) Post blinds.
2) Deal three cards face-down to each player. Follow with betting round.
3) Burn a card. Deal three community cards face-up in the middle of the table.
4) Each player discards one downcard. Follow with betting round.
5) Burn a card. Deal a fourth community card face-up. Follow with betting round.
6) Burn a card. Deal a fifth community card face-up. Follow with betting round.
7) Showdown.

Note: The difference between Pineapple and Crazy Pineapple is that in the former, the discard precedes the first three community cards, and in the latter, the discard follows the first three community cards.

Spit in the Ocean

Other Names: Spit

Type: Community Card

Number of Players: 2 to 7

Winning Hand: Highest rank. Hand consists of the best five cards from a combination of four downcards and one community card.

Wild Cards: The community card in the middle of the table is wild as well as all cards of the same rank.

Game Play:

1) Post antes.

2) Deal four cards face-down to each player and one community card face-up in the center of the table.

3) Clockwise from the dealer, players may exchange up to three cards in their hand. Follow with betting round.

4) Showdown.

Piranha

Type: Community Card

Number of Players: 2 to 11

Winning Hand: Highest rank. Hand consists of the best five cards from a combination of four downcards and five community cards.

Game Play:

1) Post antes.

2) Deal four cards face-down to each player. Follow with betting round.

3) Deal three community cards face-up and two community cards face-down in the middle of the table. Follow with betting round.

4) Players hold their four downcards out in front. The dealer counts 1-2-3 drop. Players who opt out drop their cards while players who opt to stay in hold their cards.

5) Dealer rolls the last two community cards. Follow with betting round.

6) Showdown.

The Spoiler

Type: Community Card

Number of Players: 2 to 9

Winning Hand: Highest rank. Hand consists of the best five cards from a combination of two downcards and five community cards.

Game Play:

1) Post antes.
2) Deal five cards face-down to each player. Follow with betting round.
3) Deal five community cards face-down in the middle of the table.
4) Dealer rolls one card. Follow with betting round.
5) Dealer rolls a second card. Follow with betting round.
6) Clockwise from the dealer, each player discards one card.
7) Dealer rolls a third card. Follow with betting round.
8) Clockwise from the dealer, each player discards one card.
9) Dealer rolls a fourth card. Follow with betting round.
10) Clockwise from the dealer, each player discards one card.
11) Dealer rolls the last card. Follow with betting round.
12) Showdown.

Bingo

Other Names: Tic Tac Toe

Type: Community Card

Number of Players: 2 to 10

Winning Hand: Highest rank. Hand consists of the best five cards from a combination of four downcards and a three-card row of community cards – vertical, horizontal or diagonal.

Game Play:

1) Post antes.
2) Deal four cards face-down to each player. Follow with betting round.
3) Deal nine community cards face-down in the middle of the table in a 3x3 square (see figure).
4) Dealer rolls one random community card from the 3x3 square. Follow with betting round.
5) Repeat step four until all community cards in the 3x3 square are rolled.
6) Showdown.

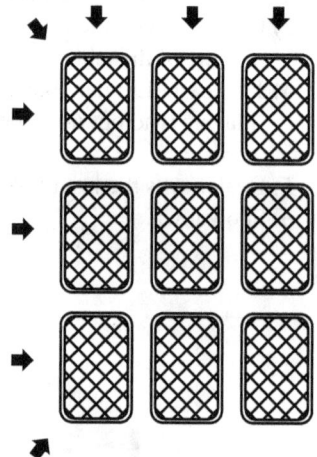

No Holds Barred

Type: Community Card

Number of Players: 2 to 10

Winning Hand: Highest rank. Hand consists of the best five cards from a combination of four downcards and three adjacent community cards (upcards must be next to each other).

Game Play:

1) Post antes.
2) Deal four cards face-down to each player. Follow with betting round.
3) Deal eight community cards face-down in the middle of the table in a 3x3 square with the center card missing (see figure).
4) Dealer rolls one random community card. Follow with betting round.
5) Repeat step four until all community cards in the square are rolled.
6) Showdown.

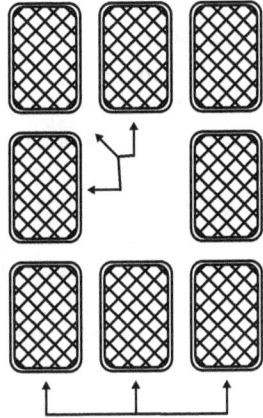

Twin Beds

Type: Community Card

Number of Players: 2 to 10

Winning Hand: Highest rank. Hand consists of the best five cards from a combination of four downcards and one five-card row of community cards – top row or bottom row.

Game Play:

1) Post antes.
2) Deal four cards face-down to each player. Follow with betting round.
3) Deal ten cards face-down in the middle of the table in two rows of five cards, alternating the deal (first card is dealt to the top row, second card dealt to the bottom row, third card to the top row, etc.; see figure)
4) Dealer rolls the first community card in each row. Follow with betting round.
5) Repeat step four until all community cards in both rows are rolled.
6) Showdown.

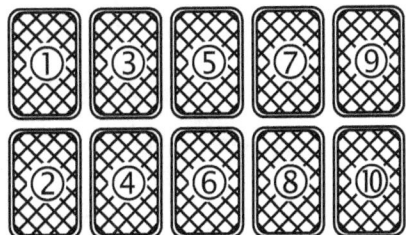

Iron Cross

Other Names: Church
Type: Community Card
Number of Players: 2 to 10
Winning Hand: Highest rank. Hand consists of the best five cards from a combination of four downcards and one three-card row of community cards – vertical or horizontal.

Game Play:
1) Post antes.
2) Deal four cards face-down to each player. Follow with betting round.
3) Deal five community cards face-down in the middle of the table in the shape of a cross – three horizontal and one above and below the center card (see figure).
4) Dealer rolls the top vertical card. Follow with betting round.
5) Dealer rolls the first horizontal card. Follow with betting round.
6) Dealer rolls the bottom vertical card. Follow with betting round.
7) Dealer rolls the far right horizontal card. Follow with betting round.
8) Dealer rolls the center card. Follow with betting round.
9) Showdown.

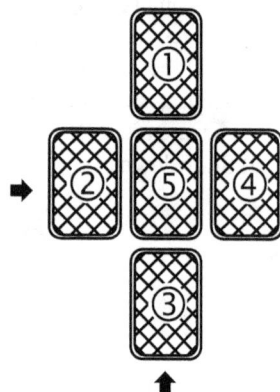

H Bomb

Type: Community Card
Number of Players: 2 to 10
Winning Hand: Highest rank. Hand consists of the best five cards from a combination of four downcards and a three-card row of community cards – vertical, horizontal or diagonal.

Game Play:
1) Post antes.
2) Deal four cards face-down to each player. Follow with betting round.
3) Deal seven community cards face-down in the middle of the table in the shape of the letter H - one horizontal row and two vertical rows (see figure).
4) Dealer rolls one random card from the H pattern. Follow with betting round.
5) Repeat step four until all cards in the H pattern are rolled.
6) Showdown.

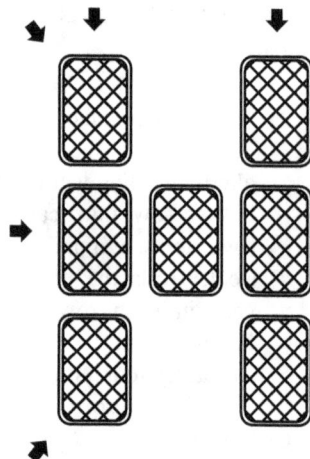

Dianna's Game

Type: Community Card

Number of Players: 2 to 10

Winning Hand: Highest rank. Hand consists of the best five cards from a combination of two downcards and three community cards.

Game Play:
1) Post antes.
2) Deal two cards face-down to each player and three community cards face-down in the middle of the table. Follow with betting round.
3) Dealer rolls the first community card. Follow with betting round.
4) Dealer rolls the second community card. Follow with betting round.
5) Dealer rolls the last community card. Follow with betting round.
6) Showdown.

Lame Brain Pete

Type: Community Card

Number of Players: 2 to 10

Winning Hand: Highest rank. Hand consists of the best five cards from a combination of three downcards and five community cards.

Wild Cards: Lowest community card and all cards of the same rank.

Game Play:
1) Post antes.
2) Deal three cards face-down to each player and five community cards face-down in the middle of the table. Follow with betting round.
3) Dealer rolls the first community card. The card is wild along with all cards of the same rank. Follow with betting round.
4) Dealer rolls the second community card. If the card is lower in rank than the previous community card, it becomes the wild card along with all cards of the same rank, replacing all previous wild cards. Follow with betting round.
5) Repeat step four until all five community cards are rolled.
6) Showdown.

Cincinnati

Type: Community Card

Number of Players: 2 to 10

Winning Hand: Highest rank. Hand consists of the best five cards from a combination of five downcards and four community cards.

Game Play:

1) Post antes.
2) Deal five cards face-down to each player. Follow with betting round.
3) Deal four community cards face-down in the middle of the table.
4) Dealer rolls the first community card. Follow with betting round.
5) Repeat step four until all community cards are rolled.
6) Showdown.

Variation: The game Ohio is played the same except the lowest ranked community card and all cards of the same rank are played as wild cards.

Whiskey Poker

Type: Combination Community Card and Draw

Number of Players: 2 to 9

Winning Hand: Highest rank. Hand consists of the best five cards from a combination of five downcards and a five-card community hand.

Game Play:

1) Post antes.
2) Deal five cards face-down to each player and include one community hand in the middle of the table. Follow with betting round.
3) Clockwise from the dealer, players may pass (keep, their dealt hand – if all players pass the community hand is turned face-up), exchange (trade their hand for the community hand by placing their hand face-up in the middle of the table and taking the concealed hand), or knock (stand pat and turn the community hand face-up. Every other player then has one more turn to improve their hand).
4) Once the community hand is face-up, players in turn have the option to exchange one card in their hand for one card in the community hand or all of their cards for the five-card community hand.
5) Repeat step four until one player knocks. Once a player knocks, every other player has one more turn to improve their hand by repeating step four. Follow with betting round.
6) Showdown.

Note: The community hand remains face-down until someone either exchanges their hand, everyone at the table passes or a player knocks.

Variation: Some games allow players to exchange from one to five cards with the community hand rather than one or all five cards.

Draw Poker Games

Draw poker is any poker game where players are dealt cards they may exchange or add to their hand during the course of play. Draw poker is the first type of poker most people learn how to play due to its simplicity. While it is not commonly found in major tournaments or televised events, draw poker is still a very popular home game with many variants.

Most draw-type poker games use antes; however, it is common to use blinds in lowball draw games which typically are played throughout an entire session of play and not as a dealer's choice type game. Step one of "Game Play" for each variant draw game lists whether it is common to start the game using antes or blinds.

Five-Card Draw

Other Names: Draw Poker, Draw High, Draw
Type: Draw
Number of Players: 2 to 7
Winning Hand: Highest rank. Hand consists of the best five downcards.
Game Play:
1) Post antes.
2) Deal five cards face-down to each player. Follow with betting round
3) Each player, in betting order, may discard up to three cards and draw an equal number of replacement downcards. This is optional – a player may stand pat.
4) Round of betting.
5) Showdown.

Variation: 1: When there are 6 or fewer players, a player holding an ace may discard the other four cards and draw four replacement cards. At some games, the player must show the ace when drawing in this fashion. **2:** The game Five-Card Draw Jacks or Better, requires players to have a pair of jacks or better to start the betting. If no player can open the betting, players discard and place a second ante in the pot for the next hand.

Psycho

Type: Combination Draw and Stud

Number of Players: 2 to 7

Winning Hand: Highest rank. Hand consists of the best five downcards.

Game Play:

1) Post antes.
2) Deal five cards face-down to each player. Follow with betting round
3) Each player, in betting order, may discard up to three cards and draw an equal number of replacement downcards. This is optional – a player may stand pat. Follow with betting round.
4) Each active player reveals three cards simultaneously. Follow with round of betting, starting with the highest exposed hand. Earliest position breaks a tie.
5) Deal one card face-up to each player. Follow with round of betting, starting with the highest exposed hand. Earliest position breaks a tie.
6) Deal one card face-down to each player. Follow with round of betting, starting with the highest exposed hand. Earliest position breaks a tie.
7) Showdown.

Note: This game starts out with the flow of Five-Card Draw and ends with the flow of Seven-Card Stud.

Threes

Type: Draw

Number of Players: 2 to 7

Winning Hand: Highest rank. Hand consists of the best five downcards.

Wild Cards: Threes.

Game Play:

1) Post antes.
2) Deal five cards face-down to each player. Follow with betting round.
3) Each player may simultaneously discard up to three cards and exchange an equal number of replacements with any other player. This is optional – a player may stand pat. Follow with betting round.
4) Repeat step three two more times.
5) Showdown.

Monkey Love

Type: Draw

Number of Players: 3 to 7

Winning Hand: Highest rank. Hand consists of the best five downcards.

Game Play:

1) Post antes.
2) Deal five cards face-down to each player. Follow with betting round.
3) Active players simultaneously declare how many cards they wish to draw, up to three cards. This is optional – a player may stand pat.
4) Each player takes the number of cards needed from the discard pile of the player seated to his or her right. If the player to the right did not opt to draw cards, that player must get cards from the next player seated to the right. If there are not enough cards to replace a player's discards, he or she must take them from the stub of the deck.
5) Round of betting.
6) Showdown.

Kings and Little Ones

Type: Draw

Number of Players: 2 to 7

Winning Hand: Highest rank. Hand consists of best five downcards.

Wild Cards: Kings and the lowest denomination card in each player's hand (including other cards of the same rank in that hand).

Game Play:

1) Post antes.
2) Deal five cards face-down to each player. Follow with betting round.
3) Each player, in betting order, may discard up to three cards and draw an equal number of replacement downcards. This is optional – a player may stand pat.
4) Each player declares in or out, in betting order.
5) Showdown. Losing hands at showdown pay an amount equal to the pot to the winning hand.

Lowball

Other Names: California Lowball, Draw Low
Type: Draw
Number of Players: 2 to 6
Winning Hand: Lowest rank. Hand consists of lowest five downcards.
Game Play:
  1) Post blinds.
  2) Deal five cards face-down to each player. Follow with betting round.
  3) Each player, in betting order, may discard up to four cards and draw an equal number of replacement downcards. This is optional – a player may stand pat.
  4) Each player that has already exchanged four cards, in betting order, may exchange a fifth card for a card from the deck. This is optional. If the last player in the betting order wishes to exchange a fifth card, the dealer burns a card before dealing the exchange card.
  5) Round of betting.
  6) Showdown.

Note: Ace plays low. Straights and flushes do not count against a low hand. The lowest rank hand in Lowball is 5-4-3-2-A.

Deuce-to-Seven Lowball

Other Names: Kansas City Lowball
Type: Draw
Number of Players: 2 to 6
Winning Hand: Lowest rank. Hand consists of lowest five downcards.
Game Play: Played the same as Lowball.

Note: Ace plays high. Straights and flushes count against a low hand. The lowest rank hand is 7-5-4-3-2, offsuit.

*Triple Draw Lowball Deuce-to-Seven

Other Names: Triple Draw 2-7
Type: Draw
Number of Players: 2 to 6
Winning Hand: Lowest rank. Hand consists of the lowest five downcards.
Game Play:
1) Post blinds.
2) Deal five cards face-down to each player. Follow with betting round.
3) Each player, in betting order, may discard up to five cards and draw an equal number of replacement downcards. This is optional – a player may stand pat. Follow with betting round.
4) Repeat step three two more times.
5) Showdown.

Note: Ace plays high. Straights and flushes count against a low hand. The lowest rank hand is 7-5-4-3-2, offsuit.

Triple Draw Lowball Ace-to-Five

Type: Draw
Number of Players: 2 to 6
Winning Hand: Lowest rank. Hand consists of lowest five downcards.
Game Play: Played the same as Triple Draw Lowball Deuce-to-Seven.
Note: Ace plays low. Straights and flushes do not count against a low hand. The lowest rank hand is 5-4-3-2-A.

Shotgun

Type: Draw
Number of Players: 2 to 7
Winning Hand: Highest rank. Hand consists of the best five downcards.
Game Play:
1) Post antes.
2) Deal three cards face-down to each player. Follow with betting round.
3) Deal a fourth card face-down to each player. Follow with betting round.
4) Deal a fifth card face-down to each player. Follow with betting round.
5) Deal a sixth card face-down to each player. Follow with betting round.
6) Clockwise from the dealer, players may exchange up to three cards in their hand. This is optional – a player may stand pat. Follow with betting round.
7) Showdown.

Assassins

Type: Draw

Number of Players: 2 to 7

Winning Hand: Highest rank. Hand consists of the best five downcards.

Game Play: Played the same as Five-Card Draw except each player that discards a Jack during the draw phase of the game has the option to eliminate one opponent in the hand.

Six Back to Five

Type: Draw

Number of Players: 5

Winning Hand: Highest rank. Hand consists of the best five downcards.

Game Play:

1) Post antes.

2) Deal six cards face-down to each player. Follow with betting round.

3) Clockwise from the dealer, players may discard up to four cards and receive one less card in exchange. For example, if a player discards three cards, the player will receive two new cards. This is optional – a player may stand pat. Follow with betting round.

4) Showdown.

Three-Card Draw Poker

Other Names: Don Juan

Type: Draw

Number of Players: 2 to 7

Winning Hand: Lowest rank. Hand consists of lowest three downcards.

Game Play:

1) Post antes.

2) Deal three cards face-down to each player. Follow with betting round.

3) Clockwise from the dealer, players may discard up to three cards and draw an equal number of replacement downcards. This is optional – a player may stand pat.

4) Round of betting.

5) Showdown.

Note: Ace plays low. Straights and flushes do not count. The lowest rank hand in Three-Card Draw Poker is A-2-3.

Stud Poker Games

Stud poker is any poker game that combines a mixture of upcards and downcards with multiple betting rounds. Stud games are traditionally non-positional games where the first person to act is determined by the cards rather than a predetermined rotation. This type of poker is the most commonly used structure copied for variant games.

Most stud-type poker games use both antes and bring-in bets. The common forced betting pattern for each variant stud poker game is described in detail in the "Game Play" section of Five-Card Stud and Seven-Card Stud. All other games, unless noted, should follow the same forced bring-in bet requirements.

Five-Card Stud

Other Names: Stud Poker, Stud

Type: Stud

Number of Players: 2 to 10

Winning Hand: Highest rank. Hand consists of the best five cards from a combination of one downcard and four upcards.

Game Play:
1) Post antes.
2) Deal one card face-down and one card face-up to each player.
3) The player with the lowest exposed card, by suit, starts the betting with a forced bet of half the lower limit. The next bettor must complete the bet, raise a completed bet or fold.
4) Deal a second card face-up to each player. Follow with betting round, starting with the highest exposed hand. Earliest position breaks a tie.
5) Deal a third card face-up to each player. Follow with betting round, starting with the highest exposed hand. Earliest position breaks a tie.
6) Deal a fourth card face-up to each player. Follow with betting round, starting with the highest exposed hand. Earliest position breaks a tie.
7) Showdown.

Variation: In the first round of betting, some games do not have a forced bet. The betting begins with the highest denomination upcard.

Three-Card Substitution

Type: Stud

Number of Players: 2 to 7

Winning Hand: Highest rank. Hand consists of the best five cards from a combination of one downcard, four upcards and up to three possible replacement cards.

Game Play:
1) Post antes.
2) Deal one card face-down and one card face-up to each player.
3) The player with the lowest exposed card, by suit, starts the betting with a forced bet of half the lower limit. The next bettor must complete the bet, raise a completed bet or fold..
4) Deal a second card face-up to each player. Follow with betting round, starting with the highest exposed hand. Earliest position breaks a tie.
5) Deal a third card face-up to each player. Follow with betting round, starting with the highest exposed hand. Earliest position breaks a tie.
6) Deal a fourth card face-up to each player. Follow with betting round, starting with the highest exposed hand. Earliest position breaks a tie.
7) Starting with the player with the highest exposed hand, each player may substitute one upcard or one downcard for one from the deck for the cost of one chip. Follow with betting round.
8) Repeat step seven, except players must pay two chips for a replacement card.
9) Repeat step seven, except players must pay three chips for a replacement card.
10) Showdown.

Note: This version of Five-Card Stud creates larger pots due to three extra rounds of betting and charging players for replacement cards.

*Seven-Card Stud

Other Names: Seven-Card Poker

Type: Stud

Number of Players: 2 to 7

Winning Hand: Highest rank. Hand consists of the best five cards from a combination of three downcards and four upcards.

Game Play:
1) Post antes.
2) Deal two cards face-down and one card face-up to each player.
3) The player with the lowest exposed card, by suit, starts the betting with a forced bet of half the lower limit. The next bettor must complete the bet, raise a completed bet or fold.

4) Deal a second card face-up to each player. Follow with betting round, starting with the highest exposed hand. Earliest position breaks a tie.

5) Deal a third card face-up to each player. Follow with betting round, starting with the highest exposed hand. Earliest position breaks a tie.

6) Deal a fourth card face-up to each player. Follow with betting round, starting with the highest exposed hand. Earliest position breaks a tie.

7) Deal a third card face-down to each player. Follow with betting round, starting with the highest exposed hand. Earliest position breaks a tie.

8) Showdown.

Note: In step four, if a pair is exposed in a fixed-limit game, any player may bet the lower or higher limit amount. For example, in a 5/10 limit game when Player A's exposed cards are 7♥7♣, that player, or any player after him, may bet $5 or $10.

Variation: In the first round of betting, some games do not have a forced bet. The betting begins with the highest denomination upcard.

*Seven-Card Stud High-Low Split Eight or Better

Other Names: Seven-Card Stud/8, Seven-Card Stud High-Low/8

Type: Stud

Number of Players: 2 to 7

Winning Hand: Highest rank and lowest rank split the pot. Hand consists of best (highest and/or lowest) five cards from combination of three downcards and four upcards.

Game Play: Played the same as Seven-Card Stud except the best high hand and the best low hand split the pot.

Note: 1: A low hand must be ranked eight-high or lower with no pairs to qualify for half the pot. Ace plays high and low. Straights and flushes do not count against a low hand. **2:** It is possible for one player to hold the best high hand as well as the best low hand and scoop the entire pot.

*Razz

Other Names: Seven-Card Stud Low

Type: Stud

Number of Players: 2 to 7

Winning Hand: Lowest rank. Hand consists of lowest five cards from a combination of three downcards and four upcards.

Game Play:

1) Post antes.
2) Deal two cards face-down and one card face-up to each player.
3) The player with the highest exposed card, by suit, starts the betting with a forced bet of half the lower limit. The next bettor must complete the bet, raise a completed bet or fold.
4) Deal a second card face-up to each player. Follow with betting round, starting with the lowest exposed hand. Earliest position breaks a tie.
5) Deal a third card face-up to each player. Follow with betting round, starting with the lowest exposed hand. Earliest position breaks a tie.
6) Deal a fourth card face-up to each player. Follow with betting round, starting with the lowest exposed hand. Earliest position breaks a tie.
7) Deal a third card face-down to each player. Follow with betting round, starting with the lowest exposed hand. Earliest position breaks a tie.
8) Showdown.

Note: Ace plays low. Straights and flushes do not count against a low hand. The lowest rank hand in Razz is 5-4-3-2-A.

Chicago

Other Names: Chicago Stud

Type: Stud

Number of Players: 2 to 7

Winning Hands: Split pot between highest rank and highest-denomination spade downcard. Hand consists of the best five cards from a combination of three downcards and four upcards.

Game Play: Played the same as Seven-Card Stud.

Follow the Queen

Type: Stud

Number of Players: 2 to 7

Winning Hand: Highest rank. Hand consists of the best five cards from a combination of three downcards and four upcards.

Wild Cards: All queens are wild. The card dealt immediately following a queen is also wild, as is any card of the same rank. If another queen is dealt face-up, the next card dealt becomes wild instead of the card dealt after the previous queen.

Game Play: Played the same as Seven-Card Stud.

Variation: If the last upcard dealt is a queen, nothing is wild or only the queens remain wild.

Harem

Type: Stud

Number of Players: 2 to 7

Winning Hand: Highest rank. Hand consists of the best five cards from a combination of three downcards and four upcards. A player holding three queens overrides the poker hand rankings and automatically wins the hand.

Wild Cards: Kings and jacks are wild. If a player is dealt a queen the kings and jacks in that player's hand are no longer wild.

Game Play: Played the same as Seven-Card Stud.

Sequence

Type: Stud

Number of Players: 2 to 7

Winning Hand: Highest rank. Hand consists of the best five cards from a combination of three downcards and four upcards.

Wild Cards: If a two is dealt as an upcard, all twos become wild. If a three is dealt as an upcard after the two card, threes replace the twos as wild cards. This continues in sequence from four to the ace, each upcard replacing the lower valued card as wild.

Game Play: Played the same as Seven-Card Stud.

Note: As the name of the game indicates, cards to be declared wild must appear in sequence. For example if threes are wild only a four can replace the three, if eights are wild, only a nine can replace the eight, etc.

Have a Heart

Type: Stud

Number of Players: 2 to 7

Winning Hand: Highest rank. Hand consists of the best five cards from a combination of three downcards and four upcards.

Game Play: Played the same as Seven-Card Stud except whenever a player is dealt a heart-suited upcard, he or she may discard the card and take an upcard or downcard from another player as a replacement. The player who loses the card does not get a replacement card.

Variation: Trade a Heart is a game played the same except a player taking a card from another player must give that player the discard to use in place of the one taken.

Cowpie Poker

Type: Stud

Number of Players: 2 to 7

Winning Hand: Highest rank five-card hand and highest rank two-card hand split the pot.

Game Play:

Played the same as Seven-Card Stud, except before showdown players must use the seven cards to make one five-card hand and one two-card hand. The two-card hand must include at least one downcard and the five-card hand must rank higher than the two-card hand.

Auction

Type: Stud

Number of Players: 2 to 10

Winning Hand: Highest rank and lowest rank split the pot.

Game Play:
  1) Post antes.
  2) Deal one card face-down to each player. Follow with betting round.
  3) Dealer places one card face-up in the center of the table for each active player.
  4) Each active player secretly places a bet in his or her hand. Simultaneously, players reveal their betting amount.
  5) Starting with the highest bettor, each player selects one of the upcards from the center of the table and places his or her bet into the pot.
  6) Repeat steps 3-5 two more times.
  7) Deal one card face-down to each active player. Follow with betting round.
  8) Clockwise from the dealer, players declare high, low or both. Follow betting round.
  9) Showdown.

Note: 1: When players reveal their secret bet, in the event of a tie, the player(s) to the left of the dealer selects the first upcard from the center of the table. **2:** Ace plays high and low. Straights and flushes do not count against a low hand. **3:** It is possible for one player to hold the best high hand as well as the best low hand and scoop the entire pot.

Mexican Stud

Type: Stud

Number of Players: 2 to 10

Winning Hand: Highest rank. Hand consists of the best five cards from a combination of four upcards and one downcard.

Game Play:
  1) Post antes.
  2) Deal two cards face-down to each player.
  3) Each player simultaneously rolls over one card. Follow with betting round.
  4) Repeat steps 2 and 3 until each active player has four upcards and one downcard.
  5) Showdown.

Variation: In some games each player's last remaining downcard is played as a wild card.

Kings

Type: Stud
Number of Players: 2 to 10
Winning Hand: Highest rank and lowest rank split the pot.
Wild Cards: Kings
Game Play:

1) Post antes.
2) Deal one card face-down to each player.
3) The top card of the deck is offered to the first player seated to the left of the dealer. The player may accept or reject the card. If it is a king, the player must accept the card. If the player accepts the card, the next player seated to his or her left is offered the next top card on the deck. If the player rejects the card, the next player seated to his or her left is offered the same card.
4) Play continues around the table and each player has the option to accept or reject a card.
5) The players who rejected the offered card are each dealt one card face-up which they must accept. Follow with betting round.
6) Repeat steps 3-5 until each active player has five cards.
7) Clockwise from the dealer, players declare high, low or both. Follow with betting round.
8) Showdown.

Note: 1: Ace plays high and low. Straights and flushes do not count against a low hand. **2:** It is possible for one player to hold the best high hand as well as the best low hand and scoop the entire pot.

Turbo Five-Card Stud

Type: Stud
Number of Players: 2 to 7
Winning Hand: Highest rank. Hand consists of the best five cards from a combination of four upcards and one downcard.
Game Play:

1) Post antes.
2) Deal four cards face-down and one card face-up to each player. Follow with betting round.
3) Deal each player a fifth card face-down.
4) Each player rolls one of the downcards.
5) Clockwise from the dealer, each player discards one downcard. Follow with betting round.
6) Repeat steps 3-5 until each active player is left with four cards face-up and one card face-down. Follow with betting round.
7) Showdown.

Wallaby

Type: Stud

Number of Players: 2 to 8

Winning Hand: Highest rank. Hand consists of the five best cards from a combination of four upcards and one downcard.

Game Play:

1) Post antes.
2) Deal two cards face-down to each player. Follow with betting round.
3) Deal two cards face-up to each player. Follow with betting round.
4) Deal a third card face-up to each player. Follow with betting round.
5) Deal a fourth card face-up to each player. Follow with betting round.
6) Showdown using only one of the two downcards.

Alligator Stud

Type: Stud

Number of Players: 2 to 8

Winning Hand: Highest rank. Hand consists of the five best cards from a combination of five upcards and one downcard.

Game Play:

1) Post antes.
2) Deal one card face-down and one card face-up to each player. Follow with betting round.
3) Deal two simultaneous cards face-up to each player. Follow with betting round.
4) Deal a fourth card face-up to each player. Follow with betting round.
5) Deal a fifth card face-up to each player. Follow with betting round.
6) Showdown.

Baseball

Type: Stud

Number of Players: 2 to 7

Winning Hand: Highest rank. Hand consists of the best five cards from a combination of three downcards and four upcards.

Wild Cards: Threes and nines are wild.

Game Play: Played the same as Seven-Card Stud, except any player who is dealt a four face-up receives an additional card face-down.

Note: Players dealt a four(s) face-up will have a higher combination of cards to make the best five-card poker hand.

Variation: Some games charge players for the additional card they receive when a four is dealt.

Midnight Baseball

Other Names: Night Baseball, Blind Baseball

Type: Stud

Number of Players: 2 to 7

Winning Hand: Highest rank. Hand consists of the best five cards rolled.

Wild Cards: Threes and nines are wild. A player may buy an additional card for a predetermined amount when a four is rolled.

Game Play:
1) Post antes.
2) Deal seven cards face-down to each player and turn up the top card on the deck.
3) Player to the left of the dealer rolls over cards from his or her seven downcards until the top card of the deck is beat. Follow with betting round.
4) The next player to the left rolls cards until he beats the last player's hand. Follow with betting round.
5) Play continues clockwise around the table with betting after each player rolls. If a player rolls all seven cards and does not beat the high hand, that player is out.
6) Showdown is when all cards are rolled.

English Stud

Type: Stud

Number of Players: 2 to 6

Winning Hand: Highest rank. Hand consists of the best five cards from a combination of upcards and downcards.

Game Play:

1) Post antes.
2) Deal two cards face-down and one card face-up to each player. Follow with betting round.
3) Deal a second card face-up to each player. Follow with betting round.
4) Deal a third card face-up to each player. Follow with betting round.
5) Clockwise from the dealer, each player may exchange one upcard or one downcard. The new cards are dealt the same way – upcards are dealt up and downcards are dealt down.
6) Deal one card face-up to each player. Follow with betting round.
7) Each player may exchange another upcard or downcard. Follow with betting round.
8) Showdown.

Note: During the exchange round, players may choose not to exchange cards.

The Good, the Bad and the Ugly

Type: Stud

Number of Players: 2 to 7

Winning Hand: Highest rank. Hand consists of the best five cards from a combination of upcards and downcards.

Wild Cards: The first rolled card and all cards of the same rank.

Game Play:

1) Post antes.
2) Deal two cards face-down and one card face-up to each player. Follow with betting round.
3) Deal a second card face-up to each player. Follow with betting round.
4) Deal three cards face-down in the middle of the table, known as the good, the bad and the ugly cards.
5) Roll the first card. This card, along with cards of the same rank, are wild. Follow with betting round.
6) Roll the second card. This card, along with cards of the same rank, must be discarded. Follow with betting round.
7) Roll the third card. Any player holding a card of this rank must fold. Follow with betting round.
8) Showdown.

The Price is Right

Other Names: Grocery Shopping

Type: Stud

Number of Players: 2 to 7

Winning Hand: Highest rank and lowest rank split the pot.

Game Play:

1) Post antes.
2) Deal two cards face-down to each player.
3) Deal two cards face-up in the middle of the table.
4) Clockwise from the dealer, each player may purchase a card in the following manner: the upcard on the dealer's left cost the player one betting unit, the upcard on the dealer's right cost two betting units, and the card on the top of the deck cost five units. If the left card is purchased, the right card takes its place and the card on top of the deck is turned up and placed where the right card was. If the right card is purchased, the left card takes its place and the card on top of the deck is turned up and placed where the left card was. If the card on top of the deck is purchased, it is dealt face-down to the player. Follow with betting round.
5) This continues until all players have seven cards. Players must continue to purchase cards, even with a pat hand. A round of betting occurs after each round of purchased cards.
6) Players must declare high, low or both. Follow with betting round.
7) Showdown.

Note: 1: A betting unit must be defined before the start of the game. **2:** Ace plays high and low. Straights and flushes do not count against a low hand. **3:** It is possible for one player to hold the best high hand as well as the best low hand and scoop the entire pot.

Wall Street

Type: Stud

Number of Players: 2 to 7

Winning Hand: Highest rank and lowest rank split the pot.

Game Play:

1) Post antes.
2) Deal two cards face-down and one card face-up to each player.
3) Deal four cards face-up in the middle of the table.
4) Clockwise from the dealer, each player may purchase a card in the following manner: the upcard on the dealer's far left cost the player one betting unit, the next card cost two betting units, the next card cost three betting units, and the

card on the dealer's far right cost four betting units. If a player does not wish to purchase a card, he or she may take an upcard off the top of the deck for free. If a player does purchase a card, that card is replaced by the top card of the deck.

5) This continues until all players have four cards face-up.
6) Deal each player one card face-down. Follow with betting round.
7) Players must declare high, low or both. Follow with betting round.
8) Showdown.

Note: 1: A betting unit must be defined before the start of the game. **2:** Ace plays high and low. Straights and flushes do not count against a low hand. **3:** It is possible for one player to hold the best high hand as well as the best low hand and scoop the entire pot.

Want it? Want it? Got it!

Type: Stud
Number of Players: 2 to 7
Winning Hand: Highest rank and lowest rank split the pot.
Game Play:

1) Post antes.
2) Deal two cards face-down and one card face-up to each player.
3) The dealer offers the first person to the left the card face-up on the top of the deck. The player may accept the card or pass to the next player. The next player may accept the card or pass it to the next player. The third player must accept the card if it was passed twice. Once a card is accepted or forced on a player, the next player yet to get a card has the first option. This continues until all players have two cards face-up. Follow with betting round.
4) The dealer offers the card face-up on the top of the deck to the next person
5) This continues until all players have four cards face-up.
6) Deal each player a third card face-down. Follow with betting round.
7) Players must declare high, low or both. Follow with betting round.
8) Showdown.

Note: 1: A betting unit must be defined before the start of the game. **2:** Ace plays high and low. Straights and flushes do not count against a low hand. **3:** It is possible for one player to hold the best high hand as well as the best low hand and scoop the entire pot.

Eight-Card Stud

Type: Stud

Number of Players: 2 to 7

Winning Hand: Highest rank. Hand consists of the best five cards from a combination of three downcards and five upcards.

Game Play:

1) Post antes.
2) Deal two cards face-down and one card face-up to each player.
3) The player with the lowest exposed card, by suit, starts the betting with a forced bet of half the lower limit. The next bettor must complete the bet, raise a completed bet or fold.
4) Deal a second card face-up to each player. Follow with round of betting, starting with the highest exposed hand. Earliest position breaks a tie.
5) Deal a third card face-up to each player. Follow with round of betting, starting with the highest exposed hand. Earliest position breaks a tie.
6) Deal a fourth card face-up to each player. Follow with round of betting, starting with the highest exposed hand. Earliest position breaks a tie.
7) Deal a fifth card face-up to each player. Follow with round of betting, starting with the highest exposed hand. Earliest position breaks a tie.
8) Deal one card face-down to each player. Follow with round of betting, starting with the highest exposed hand. Earliest position breaks a tie.
9) Showdown.

Variation: In the first round of betting, some games do not have a forced bet. The betting begins with the highest denomination upcard.

4-4-4

Type: Stud

Number of Players: 2 to 7

Winning Hand: Highest rank. Hand consists of the best five cards from a combination of four downcards and four upcards.

Wild Cards: Fours

Game Play:

1) Post antes.
2) Deal four cards face-down and one card face-up to each player. Follow with betting round.
3) Deal a second card face-up to each player. Follow with betting round.
4) Deal a third card face-up to each player. Follow with betting round.
5) Deal a fourth card face-up to each player. Follow with betting round.
6) Showdown.

Three to Five

Type: Stud
Number of Players: 2 to 10
Winning Hand: Highest rank. Hand consists of best five downcards.
Game Play:
1) Post antes.
2) Deal three cards face-down to each player.
3) Players who opt to stay in secretly place a chip in their hand. Players who opt to fold do not place a chip in their hand, but close their fist so that players are not aware of who is in or out.
4) Players simultaneously open their hands. Players holding chips are in and players without a chip are out.
5) Deal two cards face-down to each active player.
6) Showdown. The player with the best five-card poker hand wins the antes and players who stayed in and lost must match the amount of money in the pot. The pot continues to grow each hand until only one player remains and wins the entire pot.

Double Revenge

Type: Stud
Number of Players: 2 to 10
Winning Hand: Highest rank. Hand consists of best five cards out of seven downcards.
Game Play:
1) Post antes.
2) Deal three cards face-down to each player.
3) Players who opt to stay in secretly place a chip in their hand. Players who opt to fold do not place a chip in their hand, but close their fist so that players are not aware of who is in or out.
4) Players simultaneously open their hands. Players holding chips are in and players without a chip are out.
5) Deal two cards face-down to each active player.
6) Active players declare again by following step three and four. Players who opt out at this point must match half the amount of money in the pot.
7) Deal two final cards face-down to each active player.
8) Showdown. The player with the best five-card poker hand wins the antes. Players who stayed in and lost must match the amount of money in the pot. The pot continues to grow each hand until only one player remains and wins the entire pot.

Miscellaneous Poker Games

Games that do not fall into one of the three common types of poker (community, draw or stud) can be considered miscellaneous poker games. Many games of this nature veer far from the common structure of a poker game, yet use the same basic hand ranking system and therefore can still be classified as poker games.

Many of the miscellaneous poker games use antes; however, some games of this nature do not use antes or blind bets. Instead, some of the games are match-pot games where the action is stimulated by the growth of the pot and some require players to pay a predetermined amount when they lose. The distinction is made in the "Game Play" section of each game.

Guts

Type: Miscellaneous
Number of Players: 26
Winning Hand: Highest rank. Hand consists of the best two cards.
Game Play:
1) Post antes.
2) Deal two cards face-down to each player.
3) Players who opt to stay in secretly place a chip in their hand. Players who opt to fold do not place a chip in their hand, but close their fist so that players are not aware of who is in or out.
4) Players simultaneously open their hands. Players holding chips are in and players without a chip are out.
5) Showdown. The player with the best two-card poker hand wins the antes. Players who stayed in and lost must match the amount of money in the pot. The pot continues to grow each hand until only one player remains and wins the entire pot.

Note: The best possible hand is A-A.

Variation: To encourage action, institute a rule that states if all players opt out of the hand all cards are revealed and the player with the best two-card poker hand must match the pot.

Anaconda

Other Names: Pass the Trash

Type: Miscellaneous

Number of Players: 2 to 7

Winning Hand: Highest rank. Hand consists of the best five downcards.

Game Play:

1) Post antes.
2) Deal seven cards face-down to each player. Follow with betting round.
3) Each active player must pass three cards to the player to the left. Follow with betting round
4) Each active player must pass two cards to the player to the left. Follow with betting round
5) Each active player must pass one card to the player to the left. Follow with betting round
6) Clockwise from the dealer, players must discard two cards and place the remaining five cards face-down in front of him or her.
7) Clockwise from the dealer, players must roll one card each. Follow with a betting round.
8) Players continue by repeating step seven until all the cards have been rolled.
9) Showdown.

Howdy Doody

Type: Miscellaneous

Number of Players: 2 to 7

Winning Hand: Highest rank and lowest rank split the pot

Wild Cards: Threes and kings.

Game Play: Played the same as Anaconda except the highest hand and the lowest hand split the pot. Additionally, in Howdy Doody, threes are wild cards when used to win the high hand and kings are wild cards when used to win the low hand.

Indian Poker

Type: Miscellaneous

Number of Players: 2 to 10

Winning Hand: Highest rank. Hand consists of the best five cards from a combination of one blind card on the player's forehead and four upcards.

Game Play:

1) Post antes.
2) Deal one card face-down to each player. Without peeking at the card, each player places the card on their forehead so the other players can see the face of the card.
3) Deal one card face-up to each player. Follow with betting round.
4) Deal a second card face-up to each player. Follow with betting round.
5) Deal a third card face-up to each player. Follow with betting round.
6) Deal a fourth card face-up to each player. Follow with betting round.
7) Showdown.

Variation: The simplistic version of this game is one-card poker where each player is only dealt the card placed on their forehead. This version has only one round of betting followed by showdown.

Blind Man's Bluff

Type: Miscellaneous

Number of Players: 2 to 10

Winning Hand: Highest rank. Hand consists of the best five cards from a combination of two blind cards on the player's forehead and five community cards.

Game Play:

1) Post antes.
2) Deal two cards face-down to each player. Without peeking at the cards, each player places the cards on their forehead so the other players can see the face of the cards. Follow with betting round.
3) Burn a card. Deal three community cards face-up in the middle of the table. Follow with betting round.
4) Burn a card. Deal a fourth community card face-up. Follow with betting round.
5) Burn a card. Deal a fifth community card face-up. Follow with betting round.
6) Showdown.

Chinese Poker

Other Names: Russian Poker, 13-Card Poker

Type: Miscellaneous

Number of Players: 2 to 4

Winning Hand: Highest rank. Hand consists of one three-card poker hand and two five-card poker hands.

Game Play:

1) Deal thirteen cards face-down to each player.
2) Each player separates the thirteen cards into three poker hands known as the front, the middle and the back. The front is a three-card hand, the middle is a five-card hand and the back is also a five-card hand. The back must be ranked higher than the middle and the front hand. The middle must be ranked higher than front hand. The front hand must be the lowest ranked hand. (See figure.)
3) Players place the front hand face-down on top, the middle hand face-down below and the back hand face-down on the bottom.
4) Showdown consists of three steps: First, players reveal their front hand and pay one chip to each opponent with a higher three-card poker hand. Second, players reveal their middle hand and pay one chip to each opponent with a higher five-card poker hand. Finally, players reveal their back hand and pay one chip to each opponent with a higher five-card poker hand.

Note: In the front hand straights and flushes do not count and three of a kind is the best possible hand. Tied hands neither win nor lose.

Variation: 1: Some games play with bonus payments to a winner who has three-of-a-kind in the front hand and/or a four-of-a-kind or better in the middle and back hands. **2:** Some games allow players to surrender their hand after the deal and pay each opponent one chip.

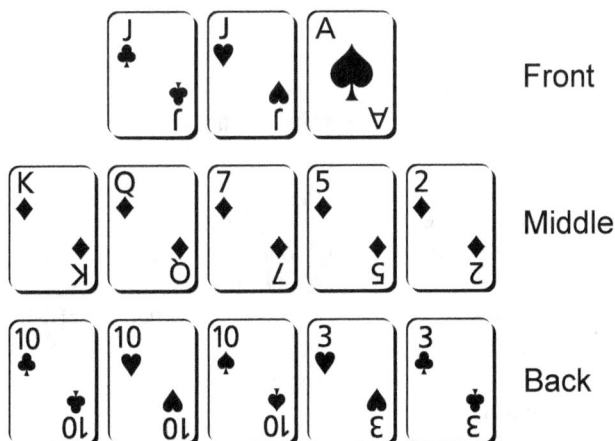

Front

Middle

Back

Pick a Partner

Type: Miscellaneous

Number of Players: 4, 6, 8, or 10

Winning Hand: Highest rank, Hand consists of best five cards from a combination of eight downcards and two upcards.

Game Play:

1) Post antes.
2) Deal five cards face-down to each player.
3) Each player rolls one card simultaneously.
4) The player with the highest upcard picks a partner. Continuing in order of highest upcard, each player picks an available partner until every player is in a team of two.
5) Each team combines their eight downcards and selects the best three to play with their two upcards. Follow with betting round.
6) Each team rolls one card simultaneously. Follow with betting round.
7) Each team rolls one card simultaneously. Follow with betting round.
8) Showdown. The winning team splits the pot.

Note: At any time during the hand, if one teammate folds, the other teammate may continue with the hand, including both upcards, and is not required to share the pot if he or she wins.

Liar's Poker

Type: Miscellaneous

Number of Players: 2 to 6

Winning Hand: No winning hand. The last player with chips remaining wins the pot.

Game Play:

1) Each player places three chips on the table.
2) Deal five cards face-down to each player.
3) The player to the left of the dealer declares what he or she believes will be the highest poker hand among all of the cards at the table.
4) The next player to the left either calls the previous player a liar (if so, proceed to step five) or declares a higher poker hand (if so, repeat step four).
5) The players cards are combined to make the declared five-card poker hand.
6) If the declared hand is made, the player who challenged the declared hand places one chip in the pot. If the hand is not made, the player who declared the poker hand places one chip in the pot.
7) Cards are redealt and steps 1-6 repeated until only one player has chips remaining on the table. That player wins the pot.

Variation: 1: To play with 7 to 10 players, deal only two cards face-down to each player. **2:** This game is commonly played using the serial number on dollar bills instead of cards; 1 = an ace, 0 = 10, flushes do not exist. In this variation each player must start with the same predetermined number of bills. A losing player places a bill into the pot instead of chips.

Mixed Poker Games

Mixed poker games are a combination of games played to comprise one entire session of play. Any combination of poker games played at the same table within the same session is considered a mixed game. Games of this nature require a high level of skill and concentration. Mixed games are increasing in popularity as players are attempting to become well rounded at numerous types of poker games. The first two mixed games included in this section are the most common combination and both are currently played at the World Series of Poker.

The betting structure for mixed games changes as each game at the table changes. Refer to the individual game directions for playing each portion of a mixed game. When a game ends that uses blinds, the dealer button remains in the same place so that the blinds pick up in the place they left off once play returns to a blind game. Most mixed games use fixed-limit betting.

*H.O.R.S.E.

Type: Mixed game that consists of five variant poker games
Number of Players: 2 to 7
Winning Hand: Varies depending on which game is in play
Game Play:
   1) Follow the directions for Texas Hold 'Em.
   2) Follow the directions for Omaha.
   3) Follow the directions for Razz.
   4) Follow the directions for Seven-Card Stud.
   5) Follow the directions for Seven-Card Stud High-Low Split Eight or Better.
Note: Intervals between each game should be a predetermined amount of time, a set number of hands or one rotation around the table.

*S.H.O.E.

Other Names: H.O.S.E

Type: Mixed game that consists of four variant poker games

Number of Players: 2 to 7

Winning Hand: Varies depending on which game is in play

Game Play:

1) Follow the directions for Seven-Card Stud.
2) Follow the directions for Texas Hold 'Em.
3) Follow the directions for Omaha.
4) Follow the directions for Seven-Card Stud High-Low Split Eight or Better.

Note: Intervals between each game should be a predetermined amount of time, a set number of hands or one rotation around the table.

Dealer's Choice

Type: Mixed game that consists of an unlimited number of variant poker games

Number of Players: 2 to 7

Winning Hand: Varies depending on which game is in play

Game Play:

1) The dealer announces the variant game.
2) Follow the directions for the game selected.
3) The cards are gathered and handed to the next dealer or person responsible for shuffling.
4) Repeat steps 1-3 throughout the course of the game.

Note: Dealer intervals should be announced before starting. Some games require the deal to pass at the end of each hand whereas other games allow one dealer to deal an entire rotation before passing the deal.

Creating New Variant Games

New variants of poker can be created by adding the following elements to any of the games included in this chapter:

- Declare any card or suit wild. Note: the addition of more than four wildcards in a game increases the luck factor and while that may create additional action in a game, it also takes a certain level of skill out of the game.
- Add a joker as a wild card or bug.
- Declare any card a kill card so that when it is dealt to a player, that player's hand is automatically dead.
- Create variant hands such as four-flush, all red flush which can include diamonds and hearts, five face cards wins, etc.
- Charge players for additional cards.
- Make the game a high-low split game and/or add an eight low qualifier.
- Change the ranking of cards.
- Add or remove betting rounds.
- Add drawing rounds or rounds where cards are traded with opponents.
- Use a stripped deck of cards. Instead of a standard 52 deck of cards, remove certain cards from play before the start of the game.

POKER GLOSSARY

Act

To check, call, bet, raise or fold in a poker game.

Action

When a player checks, calls, bets, raises or folds in a poker hand.

Action Game

A slang term for a lively poker game that has several players involved in each pot betting, raising and in general risking a lot of money.

Active Player

A player that is involved in a poker hand.

Add On

An additional stack of chips that each player has the option to buy at the end of the re-buy period in some re-buy tournaments.

Advertise

When a player reveals a lock hand or a bluff at the end of a hand in order to establish an image that he or she can later use to steal pots or induce action. For example, a player showing three consecutive bluffing hands may be advertising that he bluffs a lot in order to induce players into calling a lock hand later in the game.

All Blue

A flush that contains all spades or clubs.

All-In

To bet all of the chips or money a player has on the table.

All Pink

A flush that contains all diamonds or hearts.

Ante

A pre-set amount of money/chips placed into the pot at the beginning of each hand by every player in order to stimulate action in a poker game.

Auto Muck Hands

An option in online poker that, when enabled, instructs the software to automatically discard losing hands at the point of showdown without showing the cards to other players.

Auto Post Antes

An option in online poker that, when enabled, instructs the software to automatically post antes for players at the appropriate times.

Auto Post Blinds

An option in online poker that, when enabled, instructs the software to automatically post blinds for players at the appropriate times.

Automatic Bluff

A bluff made regardless of the cards the bettor holds, often due to circumstances indicating other players do not have strong poker hands. For example, in a Five-Card Draw game, Player A and Player B both draw four cards while player C draws one card. After the draw, if Player A and Player B both check, the situation merits an automatic bluff by Player C.

Avatar

The image or figure that represents a player in an online poker game.

Baby

A small card in the deck, usually a five or lower.

Back to Back

Two of the same cards consecutively dealt such as two spades or two aces in a row.

Backdoor

When a player hits a hand that he or she was not originally drawing at. For example, a player drawing at a straight may hit two consecutive suited cards to make a backdoor flush.

Back-Raise

When a player initially calls a bet, then reraises on the same round if another player raises the original bet.

Backer

A person who invests money in a poker player in order to split any money or prize that player wins in a game or tournament.

Bad Beat

When a strong winning hand is beat by a long-shot drawing hand or when a player's extremely good hand is beaten by an exceptional hand. In the latter situation, a progressive bad beat jackpot is sometimes offered by the cardroom.

Bankroll

The amount of money a player has earned, set aside or dedicated to invest in poker games.

Beat into the Pot

An exaggerated term that means a player calls a bet so fast that he or she places money in the center of the table even before the initial player who bet.

Beat the Board

When a player has a hand that beats the cards on the board in a community card poker game.

Belly-Buster Straight Draw

A drawing poker hand consisting of four cards to a straight with one card missing between the low end and high end of the straight. For example, 3♥4♣6♥7♦ is a seven-high belly-buster straight draw which requires a five to complete the straight. *See also Inside Straight Draw, Gut-Shot Straight Draw.*

Bet Into

When a player bets even though he or she is aware that an opponent is representing a big hand.

Bet the Pot

To bet the amount that is in the pot when playing in a pot-limit or no-limit game.

Bicycle

A nickname for a poker hand consisting of an ace-to-five straight. *See also Wheel.*

Big Ace

Holding an ace with a high side card such as a jack, queen or king.

Big Blind

The larger amount of the two bets posted at the start of each hand by the player seated two places to the left of the designated dealer in a game using blinds.

Big Dog

A player that is statistically behind and has a slight chance of winning the hand. *See also Underdog.*

Big Full

The highest full house possible in a hand.

Big Hand

A very good pat hand or drawing hand that has a good chance of winning the pot. For example, in a community card poker game K♠K♦ and Q♥J♥ would both be considered big hands to a flop of 10♥K♥7♦.

Big Stack

The player with the most chips at the table.

Blank

A card that does not help or hurt any of the active hands.

Blind

A bet made prior to the start of each hand, usually by the two players seated to the left of the dealer, to stimulate action in certain poker games.

Bluff

When a player bets a losing hand in order to convince other players that it is a winning hand.

Board

1: The cards that are dealt face-up in a community card poker game. **2:** A player waitlist.

Boat

A nickname for a full house. *See also Full House.*

Bounty

Money that is awarded to a player when he or she knocks a predetermined player out of a tournament.

Boxed Card

A card in the stub of the dealer's deck that is facing the wrong way, making it visible to the players.

Brick and Mortar

Term used for an actual casino versus a virtual card game online.

Bring-in Bet or Bring-it-in-For

A forced bet used primarily in stud poker games to stimulate action. It is a percentage of a full bet that must be made on the first betting round by the player dealt the highest or lowest upcard, depending on the variant game. *See also Forced Bet.*

Broadway

A nickname for a poker hand that consists of 10-J-Q-K-A of any suit.

Broken Board

Refers to a random flop in a community card poker game with no pairs, suited cards that could make a flush, or connected cards that could make a straight.

Broomcorn's Uncle

A nickname for a player who antes or blinds himself or herself broke.

Brush

A casino employee responsible for greeting players, maintaining poker waitlists, starting and announcing new games, setting up players with chips, escorting players to new tables and brushing off poker tables, which is how the name originated.

Bubble

1: A term used to describe the last non-paying place in a poker tournament. **2:** A term used to describe the last place before making the final table in a large televised tournament.

Bug

A wild card that may be used to represent an ace or any card that completes a straight or a flush.

Build a Pot

Betting and/or raising in order to increase the amount of money in the pot.

Bully

A nickname for a player who plays aggressively, especially when he or she has a large stack of chips in comparison to the rest of the table.

Bump

To increase a bet. *See also Raise.*

Burn Card

A card on the top of the stub of the deck which is discarded by the dealer prior to dealing cards on each dealing round.

Bust Out

When a player loses all of his or her chips in a live poker game or tournament.

Busted

1: A term used to describe a player who has lost all of his or her money. **2:** A term that describes when a player has been knocked out of a poker tournament. *See also Tapped Out.*

Button

A round disk placed in front of the player who is the designated dealer in a game where there is an actual house dealer. The disk rotates clockwise to the next player at the end of each hand. *See also Dealer Button, Puck.*

Buy-In

The amount of money a player pays to enter a tournament or buy chips for a live poker game.

Buy the Button

A rule in some poker games using blinds that allows a player coming to the table in the position left of the blinds to pay the small and big blind in order to be dealt a hand. The player who paid the blind amount would then receive the button on the next hand dealt instead of having to wait until the button is moved to the next eligible player before receiving a hand.

Cage

The place where players can exchange cash for chips and chips for cash.

Call

To match the betting amount.

Calling Station

A nickname for a player who calls almost any bet and is difficult to bluff.

Calling the Clock

Requesting the dealer place a time limit on a player that is taking an excessive amount of time to act on a hand.

Capping

The action of making the last permitted raise in a betting round.

Card Rack

A nickname for a player who is dealt a lot of good cards.

Cards Speak

1: A rule in most cardrooms that states once the cards are turned face-up at showdown, the dealer determines the winning poker hand based on the cards, regardless of a player verbally declaring a hand. **2:** A form of high-low poker where players are not required to declare high or low.

Case Card

The last specific ranked card in a deck. For example, Player A holds 4♥4♣ and Player B holds 5♦5♠, the board reads 4♠5♥9♥K♦4♦. Player A caught the case four on the end to win the pot.

Cash

A slang term for when a player finishes in a paying position in a poker tournament.

Cash Game

A standard poker game that is not a tournament or a freeze out. *See also Live Game, Ring Game.*

Catch Perfect

To hit a specific card that completes a drawing hand.

Caught Speeding

When a player is caught in a bluff.

Change Gears

When a player adjusts his or her style of play to fit the conditions of the game such as playing tight at a full table and loose when the game becomes short-handed.

Chase

Calling a bet(s) in order to complete a drawing hand.

Check

> **1:** An action on a betting round that indicates a player wishes to pass the option to bet, yet remain in the hand. **2:** A chip. *See also Chip.*

Check Blind or Check Dark

> To check without looking at the hand.

Check Out

> When a player folds a hand even though he or she is not facing a bet.

Check-Raise

> To check initially, then raise if another player bets on the same betting round.

Chip

> A token that is used to represent money in a poker game.

Chip Race

> A high-card contest used during a poker tournament after chips are colored up. The contest entails dealing each player an upcard for each odd chip presented. The dealer then adds the number of odd chips, presents an equivalent amount of chips of a higher denomination and awards the higher valued chip to the player(s) dealt the highest upcard. For example, if there are ten odd chips valued at $5 each, two $25 chips are presented, ten upcards are dealt and the two players showing the highest upcard each receive one of the $25 chips.

Chip Runner

> A cardroom employee who assists the players in obtaining chips.

Chop

> **1:** To split the pot or prize pool based on a tie, high-low split game or player agreement. **2:** In a live poker game using blinds, when players seated in the blind positions agree to take back their respective blinds when all other players at the table fold. **3:** Exchanging a chip for chips of a smaller denomination.

Clubs

> One of the four suits in a standard deck of playing cards. Each standard deck is comprised of thirteen club-suited cards.

Coffeehousing

> To make comments or ask questions during the play of a hand in an effort to gain information about an opponent's hand or to deceive an opponent.

Cold Call or Call Cold

> When a player calls a bet and a raise with little or no money invested in the pot.

Cold Deck

1: A form of cheating that entails prearranging the cards so that specific players are dealt specific cards. **2:** A period of time during which few good poker hands are dealt.

Collusion

When players work as a team to cheat other players in a game.

Color Up

To exchange lower valued chips for chips of a higher denomination in order to reduce the number of chips a player has at the table, yet not reduce actual value.

Come Over the Top

The action of raising or reraising another player.

Community Card

A card dealt face-up in the center of the table for all active players to use to make the best five-card poker hand.

Complete Bluff

A bluff made by a player that has no chance otherwise of winning the pot.

Completing a Bet

1: Raising the bring-in bet to a full bet in a stud poker game. **2:** Raising to the minimum amount in a poker game when one player has gone all-in for less than the minimum bet. For example, in a 20/40 Limit Texas Hold 'Em game, Player A goes all-in on the turn for $30 and Player B calls $40 to complete the bet when there are still players left to act.

Concealed Pair

A pair in a player's downcards that cannot be seen by other players at the table.

Connectors

Two cards that are one rank apart such as J♠Q♦ or 5♦6♥.

Counterfeited

When an upcard devalues a hand that was a likely winner. For example, in a Texas Hold 'Em game Player A holds 5♠6♠ and Player B holds A♣6♦ to a board of 5♥6♥Q♠2♠Q♣; the last queen counterfeited Player A's two pair by giving Player B two higher pair – queens over sixes with an ace kicker.

Court Card

Any jack, queen or king in a standard deck of cards. A standard deck consists of twelve court cards. *See also Face Card, Paint, Picture Card.*

Courtesy Bet

When a player foolishly makes a bet even though it is evident that an opponent with a better hand will likely call or raise the bet.

Crippled Deck

A slang term for when a player holds all the dominating cards with few to no outs to improve another player's hand. For example, a player holding J♦J♥A♠Q♠ to an Omaha flop of J♠J♣9♠ has "crippled the deck."

Crying Call

When a player calls a bet even though he is certainly beat, usually out of frustration or due to the fact that he committed most of his chips to the pot. *See also Pay Off.*

Culling

A form of cheating that entails prearranging the cards so that specific players are dealt specific cards.

Cut

To separate the deck of cards in half after shuffling in case a player saw cards during the shuffling process.

Cut Card

A blank, plastic card that is used by the dealer to cut the cards after shuffling and before dealing. The cut card conceals the bottom card while the dealer is holding the deck of cards.

Cut the Pot

A percentage of money taken from each pot by the dealer on behalf of the house.

Cutoff Seat

The first seat after the dealer or dealer button.

Dead Blind

Not having the option to raise from a blind position when other players just call the blind.

Dead Button

A dealer button that is placed in a position at the table where there is not a player. This happens when a player leaves the table at the time the button would be on that player.

Dead Card

A card that is no longer playable in a game.

Dead Hand

A hand that is no longer playable in the game.

Dead in the Pot

A term used to describe a player who has no chance of winning the pot.

Deal

The action of passing cards out to each player in a poker game.

Deal Twice

An agreement made between two players in a no-limit community card poker game who are all-in after the first three community cards are dealt. The agreement involves splitting the pot in half, dealing the last card(s) and awarding half the pot to the winner. The dealer then pushes the last dealt card(s) out of the way, deals the last card(s) again and awards the other half of the pot to the player with the winning hand. The same player may win both halves of the pot.

Dealer Button

A round disk placed in front of the player who is the designated dealer in a game where there is an actual house dealer. The disk rotates clockwise to the next player at the end of each hand. *See also Button, Puck.*

Dealer Push

When a new dealer replaces an existing dealer at the end of his or her table shift. *See also Push.*

Dealer's Choice

A poker game in which each time it is a player's turn to deal, he or she may choose the variant poker game.

Deck

A set of playing cards, typically comprised of 52 cards or 53 cards if a joker is used.

Declare

A form of poker where each active player must state whether his or her hand will play high or low.

Defensive Bet

To make a small bet in hopes of deterring an opponent from making a large bet.

Deuce-To-Seven-Lowball

A draw poker game where each player uses five downcards to make the lowest five-card poker hand. In this variation of poker, two is the lowest card in the deck, an ace is a high card and straights and flushes count against players. *See also Kansas City Lowball.*

Diamonds

One of the four suits in a standard deck of playing cards. Each standard deck is comprised of thirteen diamond-suited cards.

Discard

The action of folding a hand.

Donkey
A nickname for an unskilled player who makes foolish poker decisions and typically loses all of his or her money to other players. *See also Fish, Sucker.*

Doorcard
The first card dealt face-up in a stud poker game.

Double Belly-Buster Straight Draw
A drawing poker hand consisting of four cards to two different straights with one card needed to complete either of the straights. For example, in a Texas Hold 'Em game Player A holds 4♣8♣ to a board of 2♥K♣5♥6♠ making a double belly-buster straight draw. Player A needs either a three to make a six-high straight or a seven to make an eight-high straight.

Double-Pop
To raise a player that has already raised the initial bet.

Double-Through
When a player doubles his or her chip stack by beating an opponent with a larger chip stack.

Down to the Felt
A slang term that refers to when a player loses all of his or her chips, exposing the table felt the chips were covering.

Downcard
A card that is dealt face-down so that other players at the table cannot see it.

Drawing Dead
When a player draws for a card to complete a hand that will not win the pot even if the card comes.

Drawing Hand
An incomplete poker hand, typically referring to consecutively ranked cards or cards of the same suit, which needs to improve in order to win the pot. For example, 5♠6♥7♦8♥ and 4♠9♠J♠2♠ are both drawing hands.

Draw Out
When an inferior hand takes the lead over a hand that was a statistical favorite before additional cards were dealt.

Driver's Seat
A nickname for a player who is in control of a poker hand or seems to have an advantage over the other players in the hand.

Drop
To discard a hand and concede the pot. *See also Fold.*

Dummy End of a Straight

The lowest end of a straight. For example, Player A holds 6♠7♠, Player B hold J♠Q♥ and the board reads 8♥9♠10♦. Player A has the dummy end of the straight. *See also Ignorant End of a Straight.*

Duplicate

An upcard dealt in a community card poker game that is the same rank or suit as one of the active player's downcards. For example, Player A holds A♠J♥, Player B holds A♥10♣ and the board is 10♥Q♠K♠3♦J♦; the river card is a duplicate card that results in a split pot between Player A and Player B, who both hold an ace.

Edge

The advantage a player has over an opponent.

Entry Fee

The amount of money a player must pay in order to enter a tournament.

Expectation

One or more mathematical calculations used to determine the probable amount of money a player will make playing poker in a specific game or over a period of time. A player may measure a specific game by dividing the number of wins by the number of times played. For example, Player A played at Foxwood's cardroom 85 times last year and booked 56 wins making his expectation to win 66% of the time at Foxwood's. For more specific salary information Player A would track his exact winnings and divide it by the number of hours played. For example, if Player A won $22,000 and played a total of 680 hours over the 85 times played, his hourly expectation would be $32 per hour. This calculation of profit/hours can be done per session, week, month as well as year to determine expectation.

Exposed Card

A card that is visible to other players, whether deliberately or accidentally.

Exposed Pair

A pair that is on the board, visible to all players.

Face Card

Any jack, queen or king in a standard deck of cards. A standard deck consists of twelve face cards. *See also Paint, Picture Card, Court Card.*

Family Pot

A poker hand in which every player at the table calls the initial bet.

Favorite

A player who statistically has the best chance of winning the pot.

Feeler Bet
> A bet that is made to gauge how opponents will proceed with a hand based on whether they call, fold or raise.

Fifth Street
> **1:** The fifth card dealt directly to each player in a stud poker game. **2:** The fifth card dealt face-up in a community card poker game, where it is also known as the river card.

Fill Up
> To make a full house.

Final Table
> The last table of players remaining in a multi-table poker tournament.

Fish
> A nickname for a player who is easy to beat and typically loses all of his or her money to other players at the table. *See also Donkey, Sucker.*

Flashed Card
> A card that has been erroneously exposed to one or more players at the table.

Flat Call
> To call a bet in a situation that would normally merit a raise.

Flop
> The first three cards dealt face-up in a community card poker game such as Texas Hold 'Em and Omaha.

Flop Games
> Any poker game that uses community cards dealt face-up in the center of the table.

Flopping a Set
> When a player makes three-of-a-kind using one or more of the cards in his or her hand combined with the first three cards dealt face-up in a community card poker game.

Floorman or Floorperson
> The person in a cardroom responsible for managing all aspects of the card games, including opening new tables, seating players and settling any disputes that may arise during game play. When a dealer yells, "Floor" a floorman will come to the table to resolve any issue.

Flush
> A poker hand consisting of five cards of the same suit. For example, 7♥9♥2♥K♥J♥ makes a king-high heart flush.

Fold
> To discard a hand and concede the pot. *See also Drop.*

Forced Bet

Money/chips that players must put into the pot on the first betting round in a stud game in order to stimulate action. *See also Bring-in Bet.*

Fouled Hand

A hand that is disqualified due to error, whether intentional or unintentional. Examples of fouled hands include an exposed hand, a hand removed from the table, a hand with too many or too few cards, a hand mixed with cards thrown into the muck.

Four-of-a-Kind

A poker hand consisting of four cards of the same rank. For example, K♥K♣K♦K♠J♥ makes four kings with a jack kicker.

Fourth Street

1: The fourth card dealt directly to each player in a stud poker game. **2:** The fourth card dealt face-up in a community card poker game, where it is also known as the turn card.

Free Card

When all players check on a betting round, allowing the dealer to deal the next card without any additional money entering the pot.

Freeroll

When a player has a lock on a portion of the pot with a redraw that could earn the entire pot.

Freeroll Tournament

A poker tournament with no entry fee often offered to promote a casino or online poker website.

Freeze Out

1: A live poker game where play continues until one player has all of the money/chips at the table. **2:** A poker tournament where players are out of the tournament when they lose their chips and are not offered re-buys or an add-on.

Full House

A poker hand consisting of three matching cards over any pair. For example, K♠K♣K♥3♦3♥ makes a full house of kings full of threes. *See also Boat.*

Gap Hand

A starting hand in community card poker that consists of cards in consecutive order, but at least one rank apart. For example, 8♥10♠ is a one-gap hand; 10♠K♣ is a two-gap hand.

Getting a Hand Cracked

When a hand that started out as a statistical favorite is beaten.

Give a Card

To check a hand, allowing other players at the table to see the next card for free.

Go South

A term used to describe when a player breaks game rules by secretly taking chips/money off the poker table in order to minimize his or her risk. *See also Rat-Hole.*

Grifter

A nickname for a person who cheats.

Gut-Shot Straight Draw

A drawing poker hand consisting of four cards to a straight with one card missing between the low end and high end of the straight. For example, 3♥4♣6♥7♦ is a seven-high gut-shot straight draw which requires a five to complete the straight. *See also Inside Straight Draw, Belly-Buster Straight Draw.*

Gypsy In

A term used in lowball that means to limp in.

Half Kill

In some fixed-limit games using blinds, it is an extra blind, one-and-a-half times the amount of the small blind, that increases the limit of the game. A kill is typically activated when a player wins a pot over a certain amount or when the same player wins two or more hands in a row.

Hand for Hand

A rule applied late in a poker tournament when players are so close to finishing in a paying position that each table must play one hand at a time. If one table finishes the hand before another table, the players must wait for the other table to complete the hand before starting the next hand. This rule ensures that one player will not stall the action in hopes that a player will go out at another table and move him or her into the money by default.

Hand History

A textual replay of a poker hand provided by many online poker websites. The information can
typically be viewed on the website and/or emailed directly to players.

Heads-Up

A poker game or hand that involves only two players.

Hearts

One of the four suits in a standard deck of playing cards. Each standard deck is comprised of thirteen heart-suited cards.

Help

A card that improves a player's hand.

High Card for the Deal

The process of dealing one upcard to each player at the table; the player with the highest card by suit is the designated dealer and receives the dealer button for the first hand of the game.

High Roller

A nickname for a player who plays for large amounts of money.

High Society

A nickname for the highest denomination of chips in a cardroom.

High Spade Bet

A side bet made during a poker game where the player holding the highest card suited in spades wins the bet.

Hit and Run

A term used to describe a player who sits in a poker game briefly and cashes in as soon as he or she wins a large pot.

Hold 'Em

Short for Texas Hold 'Em. A community card poker game where each player uses two downcards and five board cards to make the best five-card poker hand.

Hole Cards

The cards that are dealt face-down to each player. *See also Pocket Cards.*

Home Game

An organized poker game played in a setting other than a casino.

Hooked

When a player is losing money in a poker game. *See also Stuck.*

H.O.R.S.E

An acronym used to describe a poker game that consists of the following five variant games played in equal intervals: Hold 'Em, Omaha, Razz, Seven-Card Stud and Seven-Card Stud High-Low Split Eight or Better.

Hourly Rate

The amount of money that a poker player wins or loses per hour.

House

The person or establishment, such as a casino or cardroom, hosting a poker game.

Ignorant End of a Straight

The lowest end of a straight. For example, Player A holds 6♠7♠, Player B holds J♠Q♥ and the board reads 8♥9♠10♦. Player A has the ignorant end of the straight. *See also Dummy End of a Straight.*

Implied Odds

A calculation that includes potential money a player could win on future betting rounds from an opponent even though the money is not currently included in the pot.

In the Dark

Taking action on a hand without looking at the cards dealt.

In the Money

When a player finishes in a paying position in a poker tournament.

Inside Straight Draw

A drawing poker hand consisting of four cards to a straight with one card missing between the low end and high end of the straight. For example, 3♥4♣6♥7♦ is a seven-high inside straight draw which requires a five to complete the straight. *See also Belly Buster Straight Draw, Gut-Shot Straight Draw.*

Internet Poker

A term used for a virtual card game played on a computer versus in an actual brick and mortar casino. *See also Online Poker.*

Isolate

The action of betting and raising aggressively in order to reduce the number of players in the hand to one opponent.

Jackpot

A progressive prize pool offered by some cardrooms or online poker websites when an extremely good hand is beaten by an exceptional hand.

Jam

When multiple players involved in a hand are betting, raising and reraising a pot.

Joker

Two additional cards that accompany a standard deck of cards and are used in some poker games as wild cards.

Juice

A percentage of money taken from each pot or more commonly, a tournament entry fee charged by the house. *See also Rake, Vigorish.*

Kansas City Lowball

A draw poker game where each player uses five downcards to make the lowest five-card poker hand. In this variation of poker, two is the lowest card in the deck, an ace is a high card and straights and flushes count against players. *See also Deuce-to-Seven-Lowball.*

Kibitzer

A nickname for a spectator who is known to offer unwanted commentary during a poker game.

Kicker

An unpaired card used to break a tie when opponents have one or two matching pairs. For example, in a Texas Hold 'Em game, Player A holds A♣Q♥, Player B holds A♦8♠ and the board is 7♠9♥A♥2♣9♦; both players have aces over nines; however, Player A wins with a queen kicker. *See also Side Card.*

Kicker Trouble

Having a low side card when breaking a tie. For example, Player B in the previous example has kicker trouble with eight as a side card.

Kill Pot

In some fixed-limit games using blinds, it is an extra blind, twice the amount of the big blind, that doubles the limit of the game. A kill is typically activated when a player wins a pot over a certain amount or when the same player wins two or more hands in a row.

Kitty

1: The pot. **2:** An agreement between two or more players to share a portion of the money they win from each pot by placing it into a separate chip rack to be divided later. A player's pro-rata share is in play throughout the game. **3:** Money collected in some low-stakes poker home games to pay for food and drinks.

Lammer

1: A chip awarded to the winner of a satellite tournament, which he or she may use for entry into a larger poker tournament. **2:** A small plastic marker used by the dealer to indicate when a player misses a blind, requests a seat change or accepts money taken from the dealers rack while he or she is purchasing chips.

Lay Down

The action of folding a poker hand.

Leak

A slang term used to indicate a flaw in a player's poker play.

Level

A period of time during a tournament in which the blinds, antes and betting increments stay the same. A standard level ranges from 15 minutes to 50 minutes, depending upon the tournament, and remains the same amount of time throughout the tournament.

Limit Poker

A poker game where players must bet in structured increments on each round of betting.

Limp In

To call the minimum betting amount.

List

A piece of paper, display board or screen used to track players waiting to play in a poker game. *See also Waitlist.*

Little Blind

The smaller of the two bets posted at the start of each hand by the player seated to the immediate left of the designated dealer in a community card poker game.

Live Blind

The option to raise from the big blind position when no other player has raised the pot.

Live Card

A card in which no matching cards have appeared and is likely to still be in play.

Live Game

A standard poker game that is not a tournament or a freeze out. *See also Cash Game, Ring Game.*

Live Hand

A hand that is still eligible to win the pot.

Live One

A nickname for a loose player that usually loses money in a poker game.

Lock

An unbeatable poker hand.

Loose Player

A nickname for a player who plays a lot of hands and rarely folds.

Lowball or Low Poker

A poker game where the lowest five-card poker hand wins the pot.

Made Hand

A poker hand that does not need to improve in order to win the pot.

Main Pot

The portion of a pot that has been matched by all active players. Once an active player is all-in and no longer able to match additional bets, a side pot is created and the all-in player is only eligible to win the main pot.

Make a Deal

To negotiate splitting the prize or money with another player(s) remaining at the end of a poker tournament.

Maniac

A nickname used to describe an aggressive player who bets and raises most pots.

Marker

A promissory note or an IOU.

Marked Cards

Cards that have been dented, scratched or altered in any way that enables a cheater to read the backside of the cards.

Match the Pot

To add chips to the pot equal to the amount currently in the pot.

Misdeal

When an error occurs during the dealing process. The dealer must gather the cards back, shuffle and deal them again. For example, when a dealer recognizes that she missed dealing to a seated player, she declares, "Misdeal, give the cards back."

Miss the Flop

Refers to when a player's downcards are not at all improved by the first three upcards in a community card poker game.

Mixed Games

A poker game that rotates the variants played throughout the course of the night. For example, a game where Omaha is played for 30 minutes followed by Razz for 30 minutes and Texas Hold 'Em for 30 minutes would be considered a mixed game.

Money Management

The business of handling a poker bankroll and taking calculated risks to maximize wins and minimize losses.

Monster

A nickname for a very big hand.

Mortal Nuts

The best possible poker hand at the time. *See also Nuts, Stone Cold Nuts.*

Move-In

To bet all of the chips or money a player has on the table.

Muck

1: To discard a poker hand. **2:** A term used to refer to the actual pile of cards no longer in play.

Multiway Pot

A hand where more than two players are competing for the pot.

Multi-Table Tournament

A poker tournament that starts with more than one table of players competing to win. Tables are combined as participants are eliminated from the tournament.

Must-Move Table

A secondary poker table opened for players waiting to play in the main game. As seats in the main game become available, players seated at the secondary table are required to move to the main game.

No-Limit

A poker game where players may bet all of the money/chips in front of them on any round of betting.

No Pair

A poker hand consisting of five unrelated cards. For example, a player holding 4♠9♥JQ♦2♣, has no pair, queen-high.

Number Two Man

A cheating dealer who is particularly skilled at peeking at the first card on the top of a deck then dealing the second card in order to save the top card for himself or a specific player. *See also Second Dealer.*

Nuts

The best possible poker hand at the time. *See also Mortal Nuts, Stone Cold Nuts.*

Odd Chip

A left over chip of the smallest denomination after splitting a pot. The chip is typically given to the player seated left of the dealer or to the high hand winner in a high-low split game.

Offsuit

Cards that do not have the same ranked suit. For example, A♠K♥ is called ace-king offsuit.

Omaha

A community card poker game where each player must use two out of four downcards and three out of five board cards to make the best five-card poker hand.

Omaha High-Low Eight-or-Better

A split pot community card poker game where each player must use two out of four downcards and three out of five board cards to make the best five-card poker hand and the lowest five card poker hand, which must consist of cards eight or lower.

On the Come

When a player bets a drawing hand. For example, Player A holds A♥4♥ and bets when the board reads 5♥Q♥K♣. The player is betting that a heart will come.

On Tilt

A term used to describe a player who is playing poorly due to losing a pot that induced frustration.

One Pair

A poker hand consisting of two matching cards and three miscellaneous side cards. For example, 7♥7♣2♠K♥J♠ makes one pair of sevens.

Online Poker

Term used for a virtual card game played on the Internet versus in an actual brick and mortar casino. *See also Internet Poker.*

Opener

The player who places the first bet in a pot.

Opener Button

A marker used to track which player placed the first bet in a pot.

Openers

Cards that meet a minimum requirement in order for a player to place the first bet into a pot. For example, in Jacks or Better, a player must have at least a pair of jacks in his or her hand in order to open the betting.

Open-End Straight Draw

A drawing poker hand that consists of four consecutively ranked cards. For example, 6♦7♣8♥9♦ is an open-end straight draw which requires any five or any ten to make an actual straight.

Option

In community card poker games, it is the ability to raise when the opening action is to the player seated in the big blind or a player that made a blind straddle bet when no other player raised.

Outs

The number of cards in the deck that will turn a losing hand into the winning hand. For example, Player A holds 4♠5♥ and player B holds Q♠Q♣ in a Texas Hold 'Em game when the board reads 4♦6♥7♣K♣. With the last card to be dealt, player A has 13 possible outs to win the pot – two remaining fours, four threes, three fives and four eights.

Over-Bet

To make a large bet that is out of proportion to the amount of money in the pot.

Over-Call

To call a large bet after one or more players involved in the hand have already called.

Overcard

When a player holds one or more downcards higher in rank than any of the cards on the board in a community card poker game. For example, a player holding A♣Q♥ to a board of 6♠8♣J♥ has two overcards.

Overpair

When a player's downcards consist of a pair higher than any card or pair on the board in a community card poker game. For example, a player holding 9♠9♥ to a board of 2♥4♦5♣7♣7♥ has an overpair.

Paint

Any jack, queen or king in a standard deck of cards. A standard deck consists of twelve paint cards. *See also Court Cards, Picture Cards, Face Cards.*

Pass

To check if no bet has been made or to fold if a bet has been made.

Pat Hand

A poker hand that requires no additional cards to contend for the pot.

Pay Off

When a player calls a bet even though he or she is certainly beat, usually out of frustration or due to the fact that the player committed most of his or her chips to the pot. Sometimes a player will pay off a bet in order to see the cards held by his or her opponent. *See also Crying Call.*

Payout

The prize or money paid to players at the end of a poker tournament.

Perfect-Perfect

Refers to a hand in a community card poker game that wins the pot when two needed cards are dealt on the turn and the river. For example, Player A holds Q♦Q♥, Player B holds A♣Q♠ and the board reads Q♣5♠6♥A♦A♥; Player B hit perfect-perfect aces to win the pot. *See also Runner-Runner.*

Picture Card

Any jack, queen or king in a standard deck of cards. A standard deck consists of twelve picture cards. *See also Face Card, Paint, Court Card.*

Picked Off

A slang term for when a player gets called when he or she is bluffing.

Pip

The symbol(s) on the center of cards ace through ten that corresponds to the rank and suit on each card. For example, the five of diamonds has five pips displayed on the face of the card.

Play Back

To defend a hand by reraising a player who has raised.

Play Over

To play in a seat occupied by a player who is taking a break from the game.

Play Over Box

A clear plastic box used to protect a player's chips while he or she is taking a break from the game.

Play the Board

Using all five upcards in a community card poker game to make the best five- card poker hand.

Pocket Cards

A term used for the downcards a player holds in a community card poker game. *See also Hole Cards.*

Pocket Pair

When a player's downcards consist of two cards of the same rank in a community card poker game. *See also Wired Pair.*

Poker Players Alliance

A non-profit organization geared toward promoting rights for poker players and keeping the game free from unreasonable government intervention.

Position

Where a player sits in relation to the dealer and other players at the table.

Post

Placing an ante or blind into the pot.

Post Oak Bluff

When a player with an inferior hand makes a small bet into a large pot.

Pot

The accumulative total of all bets made during a poker hand, usually pulled to the center of the table by the dealer.

Pot-Limit

A poker game where players may make a bet up to the amount of money in the pot on any round of betting.

Pot Committed

When a player has the vast majority of his or her chips invested in a pot making it mathematically correct for that player to call any remaining bet(s).

Pot Odds

A mathematical calculation determined by the size of a pot divided by the bet amount. For example, Player A bets $20 when the pot totals $100; Player B is getting five to one pot odds.

Pre-Flop

The first betting round in a community card poker game, which occurs before the three board cards are dealt.

Premium Hands

A term used to describe the best starting hands in poker.

Prize Pool

The total amount of money distributed to players that finish at the top of a poker tournament. The money is typically comprised of entry fees paid by each participant minus a percentage taken by the house or cardroom.

Professional Poker Player

A person who plays poker on a regular basis for his or her primary source of income.

Prop or Proposition Player

A person paid to play in a poker game by the house or cardroom. A proposition player uses his or her own money to buy into and cash out of the card game.

Protecting Cards

The act of placing a hand, chip or object on downcards so the cards are not accidentally discarded or fouled.

Protection

1: When a player bets a made hand in order to encourage opponents to fold a drawing hand. **2:** A form of collusion that entails betting a player(s) when another player is all-in with the intent of saving the all-in player from losing.

Puck

A nickname used to describe the dealer button. *See also Button, Dealer Button.*

Put a Play On

Using a strategic poker move on an opponent.

Push

When a new dealer replaces an existing dealer at the end of his or her table shift. *See also Dealer Push.*

Pushka

A term used predominantly in the North Eastern part of the United States that refers to an agreement between two or more players to share a portion of the money they win from each pot by placing it into a separate chip rack to be divided later. A player's pro-rata share is in play throughout the game.

Quads

Short for quadruplets, it is a nickname used for four-of-a-kind.

Qualifier

The minimum requirement a hand must meet in order to be eligible to win the pot in a standard poker game or more typically, a portion of the pot in a high-low split poker game.

Quartered

To win only one fourth of the pot by tying the high or low hand in a split-pot poker game.

Rabbit Hunting

A slang term for looking at cards that would have appeared if a hand continued play.

Rack

1: A plastic tray that typically holds up to 100 poker chips in five stacks of twenty. **2:** The tray in front of the dealer that holds chips, cards and buttons.

Rag

1: A low ranked card that does not appear to help or hurt any of the active hands. **2:** A term used in a community card poker game to describe a low ranking downcard that accompanies a premium card. For example, A♥6♣ is often called "ace-rag".

Rail

A barrier used to separate spectators from an active poker game.

Railbird

A nickname for a spectator standing next to the rail at a poker game.

Rainbow Flop

In a community card poker game, it refers to a flop with three differently suited cards.

Raise

To increase a bet. *See also Bump.*

Rake

A percentage of money taken from each pot or tournament buy-in by the house. *See also Juice, Vigorish.*

Rank

The value of the number or letter on a playing card. In a standard deck, an ace is the highest ranked card and a two is the lowest ranked card.

Rapping Pat

When a player taps the table during a draw poker hand to indicate that he or she does not wish to draw additional cards.

Rat-Hole

A violation of poker etiquette when a player removes chips or money from the table during a poker game in an effort to reduce his or her risk of loss. *See also Go South.*

Razz

A variant Seven-Card Stud poker game where the lowest five-card poker hand wins the pot.

Read

To make a conclusion about a player's downcards based on betting patterns, verbal statements or behavioral indications.

Re-buy Event

A poker tournament that offers players the opportunity to buy another stack of chips when they lose all of their starting chips or fall below a predetermined amount.

Redraw

To have a made poker hand with the ability to improve to an even better hand as additional cards are dealt. For example, a player holding 9♠10♠J♠Q♠K♥, has a straight with a redraw to a straight-flush.

Releasing a Set

To fold a poker hand containing three-of-a-kind when a player suspects the hand is beat.

Represent

A form of bluffing that entails betting in order to indicate a specific hand. For example, in a Texas Hold 'Em game, when all players check on the flop and an ace is dealt on the turn, a player may bet in order to represent that he or she has an ace. In a Five-Card Draw poker game, a player may represent a pat hand by betting before the draw and standing pat.

Reraise

The action of raising after a player has already raised the pot.

Reverse Tell

Purposely performing a false tell in order to deceive an opponent. For example, Player A, holding a weak hand, looks directly at his chips after the flop in a community card poker game, knowing that gesture is commonly indicative of a strong poker hand.

Ribbon Clerk

A nickname for a low-stakes player.

Right Price

When a player has the appropriate pot odds to call a bet or a raise.

Ring Game

A standard poker game that is not a tournament or a freeze out. *See also Cash Game, Live Game.*

River Card

The last card dealt in a stud or community card poker game.

Rock

A nickname for a player who plays premium cards and rarely bets or calls without a premium hand.

Rolled-Up

A term used in a Seven-Card Stud poker game when the first three cards dealt make three-of-a kind.

Rounder

A nickname for a professional poker player who "makes the rounds" to big poker games.

Royal Flush

The highest ranked poker hand which consists of 10,J,Q,K,A of the same suit. For example, 10♥J♥Q♥K♥A♥ makes a royal heart flush.

Runner-Runner

Refers to a hand in a community card poker game that wins the pot when two needed cards are dealt on the turn and the river. For example, Player A holds Q♦Q♥, Player B holds A♣Q♠ and the board reads Q♣5♠6♥A♦A♥; Player B hit runner-runner aces to win the pot. *See also Perfect-Perfect.*

Rush

When a player wins several hands in a row. *See also Winning Streak.*

Sandbag

Checking the best hand with the intention of trapping other players into betting.

Sandwich

When an active player is involved in a pot with two other players that are betting and raising one another.

Satellite

A smaller buy-in tournament where the prize is entry into a larger buy-in tournament.

Scare Card

An upcard that appears to have helped an opponent's hand, such as the fourth card to a straight or flush.

Scoop

Winning the entire pot in a high-low split game either by having the best high and low hand or having the best high hand when a low hand is not possible.

Scrambling

A shuffling technique where the dealer spreads the cards face-down on the table and mixes them. *See also Washing the Cards.*

Seat Position

Where a player is seated at a poker table.

Second/Third Nuts

The second or third best possible poker hand at the time.

Second or Second Button

A term used in a community card poker game when a player pairs one of his or her downcards with the second highest ranked card on the board.

Second Dealer

A cheating dealer who is particularly skilled at peeking at the first card on the top of a deck then dealing the second card in order to save the top card for himself or a specific player. *See also Number Two Man.*

See

An older poker term that refers to matching the betting amount.

Semi-Bluff

To bet a drawing hand that has a reasonable chance to win if called.

Semi-Professional Poker Player

A person who plays poker on a regular basis for his or her secondary source of income.

Set

Three-of-a-kind when two downcards of the same rank match one of the upcards of the same rank.

Set All-In

To make a bet equal or greater than the amount of chips in front of an opponent.

Seven-Card Stud

A stud poker game where each player must use three downcards and four upcards to make the best five-card poker hand.

Seven-Card Stud High-Low Eight-or-Better

A split pot stud poker game where each player must use three downcards and four upcards to make the highest five-card poker hand and the lowest five-card poker hand, which must consist of cards eight or lower.

Seventh Street

The final card dealt to each player followed by the final betting round in a Seven-Card Stud poker game.

Shill

A person who plays in a poker game using the house or cardroom money in order to get a poker game started or keep a game going.

Shootout

A multi-table tournament where tables are not combined until each table has one winning player remaining. Each remaining player is then moved to a final table where play proceeds until one player wins all of the chips at the table and is declared the tournament winner.

Short Buy

A buy-in for less than the minimum buy-in amount when the requirement is waived.

Short Call

When a player uses his remaining chips to call less than the amount of the bet.

Shorthanded Game

A poker game that has several open seats, with typically six or fewer players in the game.

Short Stack

A nickname for the player with a small amount of chips in comparison to other players at the table.

Show One, Show All

A poker rule for live games that states players are entitled to receive equal access to information about the contents of another player's hand. After a deal, if cards are shown to another player, every player at the table has a right to see those cards.

Showdown

The end of a poker hand when active players turn their cards face-up to determine which player holds the winning hand.

Shuffle

The action of mixing the playing cards before dealing.

Shut Out

When a player in a no-limit poker game makes a large bet that forces an opponent to fold.

Side Card

An unpaired card used to break a tie when opponents have one or two matching pairs. For example, in a Texas Hold 'Em game, Player A holds A♣Q♥, Player B holds A♦8♠ and the board is 7♠9♥A♥2♣9♦; both players have aces over nines; however, Player A wins with a queen side card. *See also Kicker.*

Side Game

A regular poker game that is not a tournament.

Side Pot

The portion of a pot created after one active player is all-in and other players with additional chips continue to bet. Players involved in a side pot are eligible to win the main pot as well as the side pot.

Sit and Go Tournament

A poker tournament (often single table) that begins as soon as the table is full of players instead of starting at a predetermined time.

Sixth Street

The fifth card dealt directly to each player in a stud poker game, followed by the fourth betting round.

Slow Play

Passively playing a strong hand with the intention of trapping other players into betting.

Slow Rolling

The inappropriate act of holding a winning hand at showdown to briefly convince an opponent that he or she has won the hand.

Small Blind

The smaller amount of the two bets posted at the start of each hand by the player seated one place to the left of the designated dealer in a game using blinds.

Smooth Call

To call in a situation that would typically merit a raise.

Snow Hand

A form of bluffing in a draw poker game that entails standing pat on a poor hand in order to bet after the draw to convince players of a lock hand.

Soft Play

Purposely not competing against a specific player at the table such as a friend or family member.

Spades

One of the four suits in a standard deck of playing cards. Each standard deck is comprised of thirteen spade-suited cards.

Speeding

A term used to describe a player that is playing fast by betting and raising most every pot.

Splash the Pot

Carelessly throwing chips into a pot instead of stacking them neatly for the dealer and players to easily count.

Split Pair

When a player holds a pair consisting of one downcard that matches the rank of one upcard.

Split Pot

A pot that is shared between players who have the same winning hand (a tie) or a pot that is shared in a high-low poker game where one player wins with the high hand and one player wins with the low hand.

Spread Limit

A structured poker game where players may bet within a specific range. For example, in a 5/10 spread limit game, players may bet anywhere from $5 to $10 on any round of betting.

Stakes

The amount of money or prize that is being played for in a poker game. Stakes can refer to anything from $100/$200 to 80 pretzel sticks.

Stake Player

1: A person who plays in a poker game using the house or cardroom money in order to get a poker game started or keep a game going. **2:** A player who is financially backed by another person. A stake player splits half of the money he or she wins with the house or financial backer after returning all buy-in money and does not share in losses.

Standing Pat

A term used in a draw poker game that describes a player who opts to play the original cards dealt and draw no additional cards.

Steal

To win a pot with the worst hand by bluffing opponents out of the pot.

Steam

Another term used to describe a player who is on tilt or playing poorly out of frustration.

Stone Cold Bluff

When a player bluffs with little or no chance of winning the pot at showdown.

Stone Cold Nuts

The best possible poker hand at the time. *See also Mortal Nuts, Nuts.*

Straddle

An additional blind bet placed voluntarily by a player before the cards are dealt in a community card poker game. A player may straddle in order to gain a positional advantage and stimulate additional action in a poker hand. Straddle rules vary from game to game, including the betting amount permitted, the position from which a player can straddle, and the option to raise.

Straggler
A nickname for a player who limps into a pot for a small call amount.

Straight
A poker hand consisting of five cards in sequential order. For example, 7♥8♣9♥10♦J♠ makes a jack-high straight.

Straight-Flush
A poker hand consisting of five cards of the same suit in sequential order. For example, 7♥8♥9♥10♥J♥ makes a jack-high straight heart flush.

String Bet
An infraction of poker rules that entails placing a bet, reaching back for more chips and adding it to the bet without making a verbal declaration.

Stub
The portion of the card deck that has not been dealt.

Stuck
When a player is losing money in a poker game. *See also Hooked.*

Sucker
A nickname for a player who thinks he plays well, yet plays poorly and has very little chance of winning in a poker game. *See also Donkey, Fish.*

Suit
The symbol (spade, heart, diamond or club) that appears next to the number or letter on each playing card.

Suited
Cards that have the same ranked suit. For example, A♠K♠ is called ace-king suited.

Suited Connectors
Two cards that are one rank apart and of the same suit such as J♣Q♣ or 5♦6♦.

Surrender
To fold a hand and concede the pot.

Swing Hand
A hand capable of winning both the high and low end of the pot in a high-low split poker game.

Table Image
How a player is viewed by other players based on his or her style of play in a poker game.

Table Stakes

A poker rule that states a player may only bet up to the amount of money/ chips in front of him or her during a poker hand. A player may not pull additional money out of his or her pocket while active in a hand.

Talon

The remaining cards in the deck after all of the cards in play have been dealt.

Tapped Out

A term used to describe a player who has lost all of his or her money. *See also Busted.*

Tell

Behavior that reveals information about the hand a player holds.

Texas Hold 'Em

A community card poker game where each player uses two downcards and five board cards to make the best five-card poker hand.

Third Street

The third card dealt directly to each player in a stud poker game.

Three-Of-A-Kind

A poker hand consisting of three cards of the same rank. For example, 7♥7♠7♣K♦J♥ makes three sevens with a king-jack kicker.

Tight Player

A nickname for a player who does not play many hands and folds often.

Tight-Aggressive Player

A nickname for a player who does not play many hands, but bets, raises and takes control of the hands that he or she does play.

Time

1: A charge to each player, typically every half hour or hour in a poker game, in place of the house raking the pot. Often the charge occurs when a new dealer sets down, at which time he or she will announce to the table, "Time Please." **2:** What a player may say when he or she is asking for a pause in the game in order to contemplate a decision.

Toke or Tip

Short for token of appreciation, a toke, also known as a tip, is money given to a cardroom employee for services performed. Commonly used to refer to a small percentage of the pot that a winner gives to the dealer.

Top Kicker

The best possible unpaired card used to break a tie when opponents have one or two matching pairs in a community card poker game. For example, Player A holding A♠9♠ to a board of 7♣9♥J♦4♦2♠ has a pair of nines with a top kicker compared to Player B holding Q♦9♦ who has a pair of nines with a lower kicker.

Top Pair

A term used in a community card poker game when a player pairs one of his or her downcards with the highest ranked card on the board.

Trap

When a player strategically plays a poker hand to maximize the amount of his or her winnings.

Trips

Three-of-a-kind where a player holds one downcard that matches two cards on the board in a community card poker game.

Turn

The fourth upcard card dealt in a community card poker game. This fourth card is also when the betting increment doubles in a limit poker game. *See also Fourth Street.*

Two Pair

A poker hand consisting of two cards that match along with two other matching cards and one miscellaneous card. For example, 7♥7♣2♥2♠J♥ makes two pair – sevens over twos with a jack kicker.

Underdog

A player that is behind and has a slight chance of winning the hand.

Underpair

When a player's downcards consist of a pair lower than any card or pair on the board in a community card poker game. For example, a player holding 2♠2♥ to a board of 3♥4♦5♣7♣7♥ has an underpair.

Underfull

A full house that is not the best possible full house.

Under the Gun

The playing position of the first player to act on the first betting round.

Upcards

The cards that are dealt face-up that all players at the table can see.

Value Bet

A bet intended to maximize the amount of money in the pot when a player is convinced he or she holds the winning hand.

Variance

A statistical measurement of a player's positive and negative monetary swings over a period of time.

Verbal Declaration

When a player verbally states his or her intention, such as call, fold or raise to $300.

Vigorish

A percentage of money taken from each pot or tournament buy-in by the house. *See also Juice, Rake.*

Walk

When all players fold to the big blind in a community card poker game.

Washing the Cards

A shuffling technique where the dealer spreads the cards face-down on the table and scrambles them. *See also Scrambling.*

Waitlist

A piece of paper, display board or screen used to track players waiting to play in a poker game. *See also List.*

Weak Ace

Holding an ace with a low side card such as any card less than ten.

Wheel

A nickname for a poker hand consisting of an ace-to-five straight.

Wild Card

A designated card that a player may declare its specific rank and suit.

Winning Streak

When a player wins several hands or poker sessions in a row. *See also Rush.*

Wired Pair

When a player has two downcards that are paired. *See also Pocket Pair.*

World Poker Tour (WPT)

An entertainment company founded in 2002 that televises a series of high-stakes poker tournaments in 17 locations around the world.

World Series of Poker (WSOP)

A series of poker tournaments held annually in Las Vegas, Nevada to determine the best poker players in the world. The series started with a single event at Jack Binion's Horseshoe Casino in 1970. The series, now including over 30 tournaments, was moved in 2005 to Harrah's Rio casino in order to accommodate the larger number of participants.

Wrap

A term used in Omaha when a player is dealt four downcards ranked consecutively. For example, 10♠J♥Q♠K♦.

INDEX

Look For

The GAME DAY™

POKER ALMANAC™

The Game Day Poker Almanac is the reference book for every poker player! It is filled with all the information any poker player needs. It includes poker rules, a directory of poker rooms, a legal guide to poker, a complete poker glossary, and much, much more. Look for *The Game Day Poker Almanac* starting Spring 2008, wherever great books are sold, or order your copy at www.FlyingPenPress.com.

Notice to the Poker Trade: To place a free listing of your poker room in the Poker Almanac's directory of poker venues, please send email to Game Day's poker editor: Editor.PokerAlmanac@FlyingPenPress.com and ask for the "Poker Venue Survey," or visit www.FlyingPenPress.com for more information.

For inquiries about advertising in *The Game Day Poker Almanac,* send email to GameDay@FlyingPenPress.com or call 303-375-0499.

www.ingramcontent.com/pod-product-compliance
Lightning Source LLC
Chambersburg PA
CBHW062215270326
41930CB00009B/1743

* 9 780979 588921 *